CELEBRATION

CELEBRATION

180TH ANNIVERSARY
BOOK OF SERMONS
ERSKINE THEOLOGICAL SEMINARY

THE SEMINARY OF THE ASSOCIATE
REFORMED PRESBYTERIAN CHURCH

Founded 1837

R. J. Gore Jr., Editor

ETS PRESS

in association with

AMBASSADOR INTERNATIONAL
GREENVILLE, SOUTH CAROLINA & BELFAST, NORTHERN IRELAND
www.ambassador-international.com

Celebration
Rejoicing in 180 Years of God's Grace
© 2018 by Erskine Theological Seminary

R.J. Gore Jr., Editor

ISBN: 978-1-62020-846-5

eISBN: 978-1-62020-860-1

Cover Design by Brian Smith

Interior Layout by Hannah Nichols

Ebook Conversion by Anna Riebe Raats

ERSKINE THEOLOGICAL SEMINARY
Due West, South Carolina

AMBASSADOR INTERNATIONAL
Emerald House
411 University Ridge, Suite B14
Greenville, SC 29601, USA
www.ambassador-international.com

AMBASSADOR BOOKS
The Mount
2 Woodstock Link
Belfast, BT6 8DD, Northern Ireland, UK
www.ambassadormedia.co.uk
The colophon is a trademark of Ambassador

CONTENTS

EDITOR'S PREFACE   9

CHAPTER 5 ARP CONFESSION OF FAITH "OF PROVIDENCE"   11

OUR COMMITMENTS   13

SECTION ONE
SERMONS FROM THE OLD TESTAMENT

"PROVIDENCE DENIED! WHY I BELIEVE IN
BIBLICAL CREATIONISM!"   19
    Genesis 1:1-31 | *Leslie Holmes*

"A CALL TO WORSHIP"   29
    Genesis 22:1-14 | *Toney Parks*

"THE GOD WHO SEES AND THE GOD WHO HEARS IS
THE GOD WHO WILL PROVIDE!"   35
    Genesis 22:1-19 | *Terry Eves*

"ALL THINGS WORK TOGETHER FOR GOOD"   45
    Genesis 50:15-21 | *Mark Ross*

"ANSWERING THE CALL OF GOD"   55
    Exodus 3:1-12 | *Toney Parks*

"GOD'S PROVIDENCE: MOSES AND THE EXODUS"   61
    Exodus 3:7-8a | *Fred Guyette*

"THANK GOD FOR FAITHFUL CHRISTIAN WOMEN WHO
SERVE A FAITHFUL GOD!"   67
    Exodus 4:24-26 | *Terry Eves*

"PIN THE 'TALE' ON THE DONKEY"   75
    Numbers 22:22-35 | *John Paul Marr*

"ABIMELECH . . . AND SACRED HISTORY"   83
Judges 9 | *George Schwab*

"AXE AND YOU SHALL RECEIVE"   91
II Kings 6:1-7 | *George Schwab*

"ALL THE GREAT THINGS"   97
II Kings 8:1-6 | *Max Rogland*

"WHEN THE CHURCH HAS GONE TO THE DOGS"   107
Esther 4,8,9 | *Max Rogland*

"FROM WRINGING YOUR HANDS TO RAISING THEM"   119
Psalm 2 | *Matt Miller*

SECTION TWO
SERMONS FROM THE NEW TESTAMENT

"HOPE IN THE FACE OF THE HERODS OF THE WORLD"   135
Matthew 2:13-23 | *Loyd Melton*

"MERCY MULTIPLIED"   143
Matthew 5:7 | *Dale Johnson*

"DISAPPOINTED IN THE LORD"   149
Matthew 15:21-28 | *R.J. Gore*

"PRAY . . . AND DON'T GIVE UP"   159
Luke 18:1-8 | *R.J. Gore*

"A DOXOLOGY IN THE DARKNESS: TRUSTING JESUS' PRAYER WHEN FACING LIFE'S PAIN"   171
John 17:20-26 | *Mike Milton*

"GOD'S PROVIDENCE IN THE BOOK OF ACTS"   183
Acts 1:6-8 | *Fred Guyette*

"THE SECURITY IN GOD'S SOVEREIGNTY"   191
Acts 4:23-31 | *Mark Ross*

"SOLA SCRIPTURA: GOD'S MIRACLE BOOK!"   201
  II Timothy 3:14-17 | *Leslie Holmes*

CONTRIBUTORS   207
ENDNOTES   211

EDITOR'S PREFACE

THIS BOOK OF SERMONS BY the faculty of Erskine Theological Seminary is an offering, a doxology unto the Lord. Since 1837, this seminary, the seminary of the Associate Reformed Presbyterian (ARP) Church, has trained ministers, evangelists, missionaries, Christian educators, chaplains, and lay ministers to preach and teach God's Word. The Confession of Faith of the ARP Church says this in chapter five, section one "Of Providence": "God the great Creator of all things does uphold, direct, dispose, and govern all creatures, actions, and things, from the greatest even to the least, by His most wise and holy providence, according to His infallible foreknowledge, and the free and immutable counsel of His own will, to the praise of the glory of His wisdom, power, justice, goodness, and mercy." Each of these sermons addresses some aspect of God's providence.

Erskine Theological Seminary has been blessed by God's "most wise and holy providence" for 180 years! The administration, faculty, staff, and student body would never claim we have acted in wisdom or in holiness at every point during those 180 years. But we do confess this: God has always been faithful and has cared for this seminary and our beloved ARP Church. This book is both our *Celebration* of 180 years of God's providence, and our prayer for the next 180 years that we may be found faithful to the Lord's calling.

As I have edited these wonderful sermons offered by my colleagues, I have limited my editing to minor matters of grammar, punctuation, and formatting. In every instance I have tried to preserve their authentic voices. Knowing these men as I do, I can tell you that these sermons "sound like" Mike Milton and Dale Johnson. As I read a

Loyd Melton or George Schwab sermon, I hear my colleagues in their unique, God-given tone and speech patterns. All of these sermons speak with the genuine voice of their author. And, if you "listen" carefully to the text, you can "hear" a theologian thinking confessionally, a Biblical scholar wrestling with words and their meaning, or a ministry professor applying truth to our lives. Current students and seminary alumni will recognize the voices of their beloved professors.

In most instances, the text precedes the beginning of the sermon. In others, the text(s) follows a short introduction, Again, I have not altered the order of the material but have left the preacher's own structure intact. In some instances, the closing prayer was part of the service as preached; in other instances, an appropriate closing prayer was written to accompany the sermon. Special thanks to Alison Gore and Debra Meyer for their work as assistant editors.

The Faculty of Erskine Theological Seminary offer this *Celebration* to the glory of God and the edification of the Church!

—R. J. Gore Jr.
Due West, SC
January 6, 2018

CHAPTER 5 ARP CONFESSION OF FAITH "OF PROVIDENCE"

1. God the great Creator of all things doth uphold, direct, dispose, and govern all creatures, actions, and things, from the greatest even to the least, by his most wise and holy providence, according to his infallible foreknowledge, and the free and immutable counsel of his own will, to the praise of the glory of his wisdom, power, justice, goodness, and mercy.

2. Although, in relation to the foreknowledge and decree of God, the first Cause, all things come to pass immutably, and infallibly; yet, by the same providence, he ordereth them to fall out, according to the nature of second causes, either necessarily, freely, or contingently.

3. God, in his ordinary providence, maketh use of means, yet is free to work without, above, and against them, at his pleasure.

4. The almighty power, unsearchable wisdom, and infinite goodness of God so far manifest themselves in his providence, that it extendeth itself even to the first fall, and all other sins of angels and men; and that not by a bare permission, but such as hath joined with it a most wise and powerful bounding, and otherwise ordering, and governing of them, in a manifold dispensation, to his own holy ends; yet so, as the sinfulness thereof proceedeth only from the creature, and not from God, who, being most holy and righteous, neither is nor can be the author or approver of sin.

5. The most wise, righteous, and gracious God doth oftentimes leave, for a season, his own children to manifold temptations, and the corruption of their own hearts, to chastise them for their former

sins, or to discover unto them the hidden strength of corruption and deceitfulness of their hearts, that they may be humbled; and, to raise them to a more close and constant dependence for their support upon himself, and to make them more watchful against all future occasions of sin, and for sundry other just and holy ends.

6. As for those wicked and ungodly men whom God, as a righteous Judge, for former sins, doth blind and harden, from them he not only withholdeth his grace whereby they might have been enlightened in their understandings, and wrought upon in their hearts; but sometimes also withdraweth the gifts which they had, and exposeth them to such objects as their corruption makes occasions of sin; and, withal, gives them over to their own lusts, the temptations of the world, and the power of Satan, whereby it comes to pass that they harden themselves, even under those means which God useth for the softening of others.

7. As the providence of God doth, in general, reach to all creatures; so, after a most special manner, it taketh care of his church, and disposeth all things to the good thereof.

OUR COMMITMENTS

In our seminary *Academic Catalog,* we define our commitments, beginning on the second page.

ERSKINE THEOLOGICAL SEMINARY SEEKS TO GLORIFY GOD.

We are committed to honoring God in everything we do. We believe that our highest calling is to glorify and enjoy the God who made us. We believe that the only proper response to the grace of Christ is to love, trust, and obey him. And we seek, by the power of his Holy Spirit, to serve him and his Church.

ERSKINE THEOLOGICAL SEMINARY IS BIBLICAL.

We are committed to the authority of the Bible, the historic Christian faith, and the gospel of Jesus Christ. As an agency of the Associate Reformed Presbyterian Church, the Seminary affirms with the ARP Church that "the Bible alone, being God-breathed, is the Word of God Written, infallible in all that it teaches, and inerrant in the original manuscripts." The Scriptures are the standard by which we evaluate faith, life, and ministry.

ERSKINE THEOLOGICAL SEMINARY IS EVANGELICAL.

We are committed to the essential doctrines taught in the Bible and repeated in the great creeds and confessions of the Church throughout its history. In particular, we are committed to the gospel of salvation by God's grace alone, based entirely upon the redemptive work of Jesus Christ. We seek to keep this message of God's grace at the heart of our teaching and to experience its reality in our lives and ministries.

ERSKINE THEOLOGICAL SEMINARY IS REFORMED.

We are committed to the Reformed tradition and especially to the doctrinal standards of the Associate Reformed Presbyterian Church, as set forth in the Westminster Confession of Faith and Catechisms. We believe that this tradition best captures the teaching of the Scriptures. Yet we recognize that we did not come to this conviction by our own wisdom or insight, but by God's grace, and so we deal humbly, graciously, and respectfully with those who understand the Scriptures differently. We also recognize that we must continue to deepen our understanding of the Scriptures and to apply the insights of the Reformed tradition faithfully and thoughtfully to issues of faith, life, and ministry in a changing world.

ERSKINE THEOLOGICAL SEMINARY IS MISSIONAL.

We are committed to serve as a resource for the entire Christian Church to prepare students for service from a variety of denominations and backgrounds to accomplish the Mission of God in the world.

ERSKINE THEOLOGICAL SEMINARY SERVES THE WHOLE CHURCH.

We are committed to serving the whole Church of Jesus Christ. Our Reformed tradition teaches that there is only one holy, universal, and apostolic Church, to which all who confess Christ belong and whom we are bound to love and serve. It teaches us that the things that unite us with other Christians matter more than the things about which we differ. We therefore view the Reformed faith as a treasure to share with the wider church, not a cause for isolation. We find that diverse perspectives in our community enrich learning and prepare students to work respectfully alongside others in ministry. And so, while our first priority is serving the ARP Church and similar Reformed churches, we gladly open our doors to students from many denominations, and through academic programs, special events, and the varied ministries of our faculty, staff, and students, Erskine serves the whole Church of Jesus Christ.

ERSKINE THEOLOGICAL SEMINARY PREPARES STUDENTS FOR MINISTRY.

We are committed to preparing students for ministry. Because we are committed to the Church, our primary focus is on preparing men and women to serve in Christ's Church. We provide rigorous academic instruction in the Bible, theology, church history, and the practice of ministry, always seeking to apply these to the needs of the Church and its ministry. We also seek to develop students' spiritual and personal maturity, clarity about their gifts and calling, and the skills and dispositions required for effective ministry. The measure of our ministry is the faithfulness and fruitfulness of theirs.

If you share our values and are interested in studying with us at Erskine Theological Seminary, please contact us:

Ms. Robin Broome, Director of Recruitment and Enrollment, broome@erskine.edu

Phone: 864-379-6571

Mr. David Cathcart, Admissions Counselor, cathcart@erskine.edu

Phone: 864-379-6596

Dr. R. J. Gore Jr., Dean, rgore@erskine.edu

Phone: 864-378-7923

Section One

SERMONS FROM THE OLD TESTAMENT

"The creation is quite like a spacious and splendid house, provided and filled with the most exquisite, and at the same time, the most abundant furnishings. Everything in it tells of God."

—John Calvin

"PROVIDENCE DENIED! WHY I BELIEVE IN BIBLICAL CREATIONISM!"*

In the beginning, God created the heavens and the earth. The earth was without form and void, and darkness was over the face of the deep. And the Spirit of God was hovering over the face of the waters. And God said, "Let there be light," and there was light. And God saw that the light was good. And God separated the light from the darkness. God called the light Day, and the darkness he called Night. And there was evening and there was morning, the first day. And God said, "Let there be an expanse in the midst of the waters, and let it separate the waters from the waters." And God made the expanse and separated the waters that were under the expanse from the waters that were above the expanse. And it was so. And God called the expanse Heaven. And there was evening and there was morning, the second day. And God said, "Let the waters under the heavens be gathered together into one place, and let the dry land appear." And it was so. God called the dry land Earth, and the waters that were gathered together he called Seas. And God saw that it was good. And God said, "Let the earth sprout vegetation,

---

* This sermon was preached by Dr. Leslie Holmes at Covenant of Grace ARP Church in Winston-Salem, NC on November 19, 2017. Theme: The God of Providence is first and foremost the God Who created all things and upholds all things by the word of His power.

plants yielding seed, and fruit trees bearing fruit in which is their seed, each according to its kind, on the earth." And it was so. The earth brought forth vegetation, plants yielding seed according to their own kinds, and trees bearing fruit in which is their seed, each according to its kind. And God saw that it was good. And there was evening and there was morning, the third day. And God said, "Let there be lights in the expanse of the heavens to separate the day from the night. And let them be for signs and for seasons, and for days and years, and let them be lights in the expanse of the heavens to give light upon the earth." And it was so. And God made the two great lights—the greater light to rule the day and the lesser light to rule the night—and the stars. And God set them in the expanse of the heavens to give light on the earth, to rule over the day and over the night, and to separate the light from the darkness. And God saw that it was good. And there was evening and there was morning, the fourth day. And God said, "Let the waters swarm with swarms of living creatures, and let birds fly above the earth across the expanse of the heavens." So God created the great sea creatures and every living creature that moves, with which the waters swarm, according to their kinds, and every winged bird according to its kind. And God saw that it was good. And God blessed them, saying, "Be fruitful and multiply and fill the waters in the seas, and let birds multiply on the earth." And there was evening and there was morning, the fifth day. And God said, "Let the earth bring forth living creatures according to their kinds— livestock and creeping things and beasts of the earth according to their kinds." And it was so. And God made the beasts of the earth according to their kinds and the livestock according to their kinds, and everything that creeps on the ground according to its kind. And God saw that it was good. Then God said, "Let us make man in our image, after our likeness. And let them have dominion over the fish of the sea and over the birds of the heavens and over the livestock and over all the earth and over every creeping thing that creeps on the earth. So God created man in his own image, in the image of

God he created him; male and female he created them. And God blessed them. And God said to them, "Be fruitful and multiply and fill the earth and subdue it, and have dominion over the fish of the sea and over the birds of the heavens and over every living thing that moves on the earth." And God said, "Behold, I have given you every plant yielding seed that is on the face of all the earth, and every tree with seed in its fruit. You shall have them for food. And to every beast of the earth and to every bird of the heavens and to everything that creeps on the earth, everything that has the breath of life, I have given every green plant for food." And it was so. And God saw everything that he had made, and behold, it was very good. And there was evening and there was morning, the sixth day.   Genesis 1:1-31 (ESV)*

Jude, a servant of Jesus Christ and brother of James, To those who are called, beloved in God the Father and kept for Jesus Christ: May mercy, peace, and love be multiplied to you. Beloved, although I was very eager to write to you about our common salvation, I found it necessary to write appealing to you to contend for the faith that was once for all delivered to the saints. For certain people have crept in unnoticed who long ago were designated for this condemnation, ungodly people, who pervert the grace of our God into sensuality and deny our only Master and Lord, Jesus Christ.   Jude 1:1-4 (ESV)*

Two religions compete to dominate the soul of America in our time, and each is exclusive of the other. The two religions are biblical Christianity—that "faith that was once for all entrusted to the saints" (Jude 1:3). The other religion is neo-Darwinian evolution. It is the backdrop for much of what is taught in our public school classrooms. It has in fact become the *"license for immorality and (the denial of) Jesus Christ our only Sovereign and Lord"* (Jude 1:4).

In the neo-Darwinian language that often dominates education and the media, a creationist is pictured as someone whose principle aim in life is to preserve religious prejudice in spite of clear and convincing scientific evidence. That is a mischaracterization, if ever there was one. A creationist is simply a person who believes in the existence of a Creator who brought about the formation of the world and its living creatures to further His own purposes. At the same time, it is also an unfair mischaracterization to say that all evolutionists believe the same thing. There are, in fact, deep divisions among those who subscribe to the evolutionary hypothesis—and it is only a hypothesis, for in true science a hypothesis cannot be called a theory until it can be proven by repeated experiments, which is not possible when it comes to the beginning of life. Principal among these are the "micro-evolutionists" and "macro-evolutionists."

Micro-evolution is the name given for genetic changes within species. If you look at the photographs in our family album, you would quickly recognize that my American granddaughters are both taller than their Northern Ireland-born grandparents: my wife, Barbara, and me. You might say that is because their Dad, Mike, is a towering 6-feet, 4-inches tall. However, that does not explain the fact that their American-born mother is taller than her parents and her Northern Ireland-born brother. This fact is apparent not only in our family; it is clear to anyone who has traveled in Europe and the United States of America. Nothing in Scripture contradicts that possibility.

Macro-evolution, however, is different because it teaches that new species simply appeared out of nothing. Some macro-evolutionists believe these changes were spontaneous. Others believe they were continuous. How could there be such a disagreement? There is no credible scientific evidence for either position. That is just one reason why I am an advocate for biblical creationism. That is to say, I believe the creation account as set forth in Genesis. There are other reasons why I am a creationist, too. Let me explain some of them using three words.

I am a creationist because neo-Darwinian evolution is **scientifically** bankrupt. This will come as a shock to some people. Many lay people who blindly accept neo-Darwinian evolution believe science has proven it. That is not true simply because, as I have already said, it is not provable. We cannot go back to the beginning and recreate the circumstances. The rules of science for proving anything call for a repeatable experiment that produces the same predictable results every time. It is impossible to repeat the beginning of the world. For the same reason, the Genesis record is not provable.

Now, suppose that your preacher were to begin each Sunday sermon by saying, "Today I want you to commit your mind to something that is not only unproved, it is beyond hope of ever being proved." Would you come back to hear that preacher week after week? Most likely not!

Yet, that is the very foundation that proponents of the evolutionary hypothesis promote day after day before many of America's school children. They appear to have lost sight of the fact that the two foundational laws of all science stand in direct opposition to such a statement.

Let me speak about those two laws: The first law of science states that in a closed system energy is neither created nor destroyed. That is to say, nothing "just happens." When something happens, someone or something causes it to happen. Hence, everything that ever was still exists in some form. For example, you fill your car with gasoline. Then, you drive until the gas tank is empty. What happened? Where did the gasoline go? The answer is that what you once pumped into your car as liquid became gaseous fumes. Those fumes rose into the atmosphere and you could neither see nor smell them. Yet, Darwinian evolution teaches that some things happen out of nothing. Hence, it says that once upon a time, a single-cell amoeba crawled up out of the water and developed legs from out of nowhere and became a creeping creature. Next it developed feathers, again from out of nowhere, and became a flying creature, and so on. But wait, what happened, and how did it happen? Evolutionary science has no answer for that question. What or who caused these events? The evolutionist has no answer. "It just developed," is the usual response, which is a total denial of the first law of their own realm.

The second law of science asserts that physical things, left untouched, tend toward disorder. That is, things not cared for naturally fall into disarray. We have all seen those abandoned barns that lie in ruins around our countryside. Or, come with me to my homeland and witness for yourself the ruins of once-grand castles. What happened to those once-stately structures? Clearly, left untended they fell into disarray: paint peeled, wood rotted, and rocks once carefully assembled by the builders fell apart. Neo-Darwinism, however, asserts that things left alone improve. A single-cell creature became a crawler, then a walking creature, then a flying creature, then a climbing creature, and finally an erect creature with an opposable thumb. All this happened despite neglect! The second law of science says, "Impossible!"

I am a creationist because neo-Darwinian evolution is **spiritually** bankrupt. In the words of the Apostles' Creed, "I believe in God the Father Almighty, maker of heaven and earth." I am a creationist because I find that this position alone is consistent with the Bible and is the only one that finally makes good sense.

Three times in Genesis chapter 1 we find an astonishing statement that tells of the divine creation of the universe. First, this: *"In the beginning God created the heavens and the earth"* (Genesis 1:1). *Then, this: "God created the great creatures of the sea and every living and moving thing with which the water teems, according to their kinds, and every winged bird according to its kind. And God saw that it was good"* (Genesis 1:21). It speaks of the creation of life. Finally, this: *"God created man in his own image, in the image of God he created him; male and female he created them"* (Genesis 1:27).

The key word is the Hebrew verb *bara*, which means "to directly create." God created matter: *"the heavens and earth."* God created life: *"every living and moving thing."* God created humans: *"male and female he created them."* All created directly by God. They did not just happen and they did not evolve. They were created directly by God. From the beginning, it was all providence!

Furthermore, I have come to believe that God created the whole universe in six days, each consisting of 24 hours. Let me tell you why: Once again, we turn to the Hebrew text where we find a sequence of Hebrew words that confirm this. Those words, translated into English for us as *"day," "night," "evening,"* and *"morning"* strongly imply the beginning of the Earth's rotation on the first day. The use of the Hebrew word *'ehad* (meaning "one" day; then "second" *'ehad*, "third" *'ehad*, and so forth) as an ordinal number also supports this view. The Jews reckoned the beginning of a day with the evening rather than the morning.

I am especially grateful for the teaching of Dr. Jack Scott, my seminary professor of Hebrew who pointed out that anywhere these words appear in ancient Hebrew writings they speak exclusively of 24-hour days. This is confirmed by Dr. Andrew E. Steinmann, Hebrew professor at Concordia University in Chicago in his article *"'ehad as an Ordinal Number and the Meaning of Genesis 1:5,"* published in the *Journal of the Evangelical Theological Society* (December 2002) pages 577-84. Dr. Steinmann, along with Dr. Scott, points out that ordinal numbers express order (e.g., first, second, third, etc.) while cardinal numbers are used in counting (e.g., one, two, three, etc.). Some people, even some Christians, question whether this matters. "What difference does it make," some might ask, "if it was six literal 24-hour days or six periods of immeasurable time?" My response is that it matters greatly. To question whether the days of creation were literal 24-hour days is not a question of how the Earth came to be so much as a question of who called it into being. It is not a question of science but of theology!

I am a biblical creationist because biblical creationism gives my life **significance** against the scientific and spiritual bankruptcy of neo-Darwinian evolution. It will do the same for you. Now I speak specifically about providence. No other book provides such valuable statements of our purpose for human existence as does the Bible. For example, the Bible says that we are God's purpose in creation. As the creation week came to an end, there was a great covenantal decision made among the Godhead of God the Father, God the Son, and God the Holy Spirit. The Bible records that covenantal decision in these words:

> Then God said, "Let us make man in our image, after our likeness. And let them have dominion over the fish of the sea and over the birds of the heavens and over the livestock and over all the earth and over every creeping thing that creeps on the earth." So God created man in His own image, in the image of God He created him; male and female He created them. And God blessed them. And God said to them, "Be fruitful and multiply and fill the earth and subdue it, and have dominion over the fish of the sea and over the birds of the heavens and over every living thing that moves on the earth" (Genesis 1:26-28).

This covenantal statement gives our life purpose. No adaptation of Darwinian evolution will ever do that.

So, you may ask, "What difference does it make whether I believe in biblical creationism or Darwinian evolutionism?" My answer: It makes all the difference in the world when it comes to raising children. Consider this word from Solomon, reputed to be the wisest man who ever lived: *"Train up a child in the way he should go; even when he is old he will not depart from it"* (Proverbs 22:6). Earlier I said our country's future hinges to a large degree upon which shall finally prevail. In fact, the whole of human history depends upon it. Does that sound like an overstatement? *"Train up a child* (to believe he is the latest link in a chain of animals) *and when he is old* (he will act like an animal)." Why should we expect otherwise? *"Train up a child* (to believe he is the prize of all creation) *and when he is old, he will* (strive to be the best he can be for his Creator)."

You see, only biblical creationism offers humanity hope for the truth that God made you and made me, and we are the highest and best of all His creation. From Him we came and to Him we shall one day go. The Bible clearly declares that we shall each stand before our Creator to give an account of our lives. We have sinned, each of us, and we have no hope for that day save the hope that God has purchased for us on the cross of His dear Son, Jesus Christ, whose hope alone is certain. *"This is a trustworthy saying that deserves full acceptance (and for this we labor and strive), that we have put our hope in the living God, who is the Savior of all men, and especially of those who believe"* (I Timothy 4:9,10). Sinners find their only hope in Christ of whom John says, *"All things were made through him, and without him was not anything made that was made"* (John 1:3). Without Him I have neither purpose nor hope; neither do you.

Do you believe this? If you do, praise God your Creator-Redeemer. If you do not then I beg of you to run today to the cross of your Creator-Redeemer, Jesus Christ of Nazareth, Son of God, Creator, with the Father and the Holy Spirit, of all things, and Savior of the world, so you may be clothed in the righteousness that comes by Him alone— your Creator who died for you on Calvary's cross and rose again to reign with the Father for all eternity.

> **PRAYER:** ALMIGHTY GOD AND HEAVENLY Father, we praise You for Your works of Creation and Providence, for making all things out of nothing by the word of Your power. We pray that all who hear this word will believe You are both our Creator, Who breathed into Adam the breath of life, but also the Redeemer Who sent the Second Adam to bear the guilt of our sins and bring us the gift of salvation. In Jesus' name we pray, Amen.

"Men will never worship God with a sincere heart, or be roused to fear and obey Him with sufficient zeal, until they properly understand how much they are indebted to his mercy."

—John Calvin

"A CALL TO WORSHIP"*

And it came to pass after these things, that God did tempt Abraham, and said unto him, Abraham: and he said, Behold, here I am. And he said, Take now thy son, thine only son Isaac, whom thou lovest, and get thee into the land of Moriah; and offer him there for a burnt offering upon one of the mountains which I will tell thee of. And Abraham rose up early in the morning, and saddled his ass, and took two of his young men with him, and Isaac his son, and clave the wood for the burnt offering, and rose up, and went unto the place of which God had told him. Then on the third day Abraham lifted up his eyes, and saw the place afar off. And Abraham said unto his young men, Abide ye here with the ass; and I and the lad will go yonder and worship, and come again to you. And Abraham took the wood of the burnt offering, and laid it upon Isaac his son; and he took the fire in his hand, and a knife; and they went both of them together. And Isaac spake unto Abraham his father, and said, My father: and he said, Here am I, my son. And he said, Behold the fire and the wood: but where is the lamb for a burnt offering? And Abraham said, My son, God will

---

* Preached by Dr. Toney Parks at the South Carolina Christian Education Conference on July 14, 2016. Theme: God demonstrates His provisions through our willingness to obey, sacrifice, and surrender to His will. Worship is the method by which we show God our appreciation for His love for humanity.

provide himself a lamb for a burnt offering: so they went both of them together. And they came to the place which God had told him of; and Abraham built an altar there, and laid the wood in order, and bound Isaac his son, and laid him on the altar upon the wood. And Abraham stretched forth his hand, and took the knife to slay his son. And the angel of the LORD called unto him out of heaven, and said, Abraham, Abraham: and he said, Here am I. And he said, Lay not thine hand upon the lad, neither do thou any thing unto him: for now I know that thou fearest God, seeing thou hast not withheld thy son, thine only son from me. And Abraham lifted up his eyes, and looked, and behold behind him a ram caught in a thicket by his horns: and Abraham went and took the ram, and offered him up for a burnt offering in the stead of his son. And Abraham called the name of that place Jehovahjireh: as it is said to this day, In the mount of the LORD it shall be seen.   Genesis 22:1-14 (KJV)

That which is created, was made to worship the creator. Only God can take emptiness, void, and darkness and create order. God's presence is demonstrated in and through His power. God's methodical order and divine providence is evident in the visible and organized structure of heaven and earth. Only God can speak creation into existence and allow that which was created to exist for His glory. Everything made by God has a purpose. God spoke life into existence. Everything God made obeyed. Creation demonstrated its willingness to honor and worship the creator by meeting the needs of humanity.

God's plan for humanity began when He spoke! God knew what He was doing from the beginning; He provided so man's needs would be met. In this we see God's love. God recognized the usefulness of what He made by saying it was good. He then made humanity and said it was *"very good."* God expects creation to honor and worship Him for who He is, and what He has done from the foundation of the world. The providence of God is forever present through His demonstrated power and grace through redemption.

God is to be worshiped. From the beginning, man was created to worship God. In the Garden, Adam was a Worshiper, before he was a husband. He was a Worshiper, before he was a Father. Before the fall, man was in constant worship with God. The Hebrew meaning of "Eden" translates as the "place" or "presence" of God. It is important to remember that *"the Earth is the Lord's and the Fullness thereof, the world and they that dwell in it"* (Psalm 24:1). It was not God's desire that man would have to invite or invoke the presence of God in our places of worship. God is sovereign; we must stand in awe of God, and shudder in His presence. We are not big enough to invite God into our presence.

As a Worshiper, we are always in the presence of God. When we worship, we should present ourselves as living sacrifices. We should *"enter into His gates with thanksgiving and into His courts with praise"* (Psalm 100:4). As Worshipers, we are constantly glorifying God for His worthiness. He is forever to be praised. In the Garden, God was the object of our worship. Worship involves a state of holiness; worship is being obedient to God; worship is being devoted to God. Worship is being committed and faithful to God's Word.

God has always sought spiritual relationship with man. Man has fallen out of fellowship with God; therefore, God is calling us back to worship. Sin gets in the way of man's ability to give glory and honor to God. God seeks a relationship, so that He is able to enjoy fellowship with the one He created. Sin violates and separates the spiritual relationship between God and man. When Adam sinned, guilt, shame, and pride got in the way of his relationship (worship) with God. Adam became distant from God.

When you are out of fellowship with God, it seems easier to hide from God than it is to engage Him. People struggle with their prayer life when they are out of fellowship with God. It's difficult to study the Bible when the Bible study is about you. We find ourselves hiding from God, distancing ourselves in an attempt to get out of doing what we were created to do, Worship! Because of God's redemptive love, and unconditional grace, God seeks man. He called Adam; He called

Abraham; and He established a **redemptive** process by which we are able to enter into His presence. God called Adam. He called Cain. He called Noah. He called Abraham, and He is calling us to worship! Each time God called those men, He established a process and place of worship. With Adam, it was blood sacrifice. With Cain and Abel, it was the first fruit. With Noah, it was the Ark. With Abraham, it was an altar on Mt. Moriah.

God calls Abraham's name, and Abraham responded by saying, *"Here am I."* We must be willing to listen to God and answer when He calls our name. Worship is not only listening, but answering God when He calls. Worship is about being obedient; you must do as God says, and do it the way He says. There can be no "have it your way," as Burger King markets its hamburgers. No, you must be willing to follow His will. We must be submissive to the will of God. Too often, we fail to experience the provisions of God because we fail to submit to His will. Abraham was obedient, trusting, and faithful to God's word.

Worship is about making **sacrifices.** In Genesis 22:2, *"Take now your son, your only son Isaac, whom you love."* Effective and authentic worship is demonstrated through sacrificial and unselfish service to God. To effectively worship God, you must be willing to give as He asks, as Abraham did (*"Take now your son"*). You have to be willing to give God your best (*"your only Son"*) unselfishly. God didn't ask for Ishmael; He asked for Isaac. To worship God, you must be willing to show God your commitment to Him through your actions. When Abraham showed that he would sacrifice his only son, God did not allow him, and instead told him not to touch the lad, because *"now I know"* (Genesis 22:12). God saw in Abraham what He would love to see in all of us, the desire to obey and trust Him fully.

Worship is part of the **redemptive** process of salvation; you have to be willing to give up something to be saved. Worship is being in the place or presence of God, recognizing His worth, and honoring Him for who He is and what He has done in your life. *"Greater is He that is in you than he that is in the world"* (I John 4:4). That's why you need to present yourself as a living sacrifice which is your reasonable service. We must make ourselves available to God if we are going to see the blessing and provisions of God. Obedience and sacrifice are important in our lives, if we are to experience God's provisions and favor. Abraham was committed to God; he had grown to trust God to the extent that he believed God would do exactly what He said He would do! After all, God had promised Abraham before and He always kept His promise.

Worship is about surrendering to the will of God. Not everyone will understand your relationship, your commitment, or your willingness to be a sacrifice for God. There are some things you have to do all by yourself. There are some people you will have to leave behind. Abraham was committed, believing that God would provide. True and authentic worship is based upon your knowledge of who God is and what He has done for you. This is your testimony. God is seeking Worshipers. Worship is a call to sacrifice, a call to obedience, and a willingness to surrender to the will of God. God only wants your best! When you worship rightly, God will provide a Lamb for a Burnt Offering.

Abraham obeyed God. He was willing to sacrifice his only son. Abraham worshiped God and watched God provide. God stepped in at the right time; He is an on-time God. God will meet us in the midst of our greatest trials; He will test us to determine our faith; He will sustain us through our tribulations. Ultimately, God will provide for us through His only Son, Jesus Christ. It was on that same mountain, on a rugged cross, where God gave His only Son for you and me.

PRAYER: GOD OF ABRAHAM, ISAAC, and Jacob, we thank You for Your bountiful creation. Thank You for the beauty of all that You made. Your love is felt and seen in Your creation. Thank You for all that You have done, are doing, and will do for our well-being. Thank You for each and every day of our lives. I pray that the power of the Gospel would have its way in the life of each person hearing this message. Let Your will be done, in the wonderful name of Your son, Jesus Christ, Amen.

"When Jesus in the Gospels does something strange or unusual to me as a 20th century man, then I have learned to study the text even more carefully in order to understand him."

—F. F. Bruce

"THE GOD WHO SEES AND THE GOD WHO HEARS IS THE GOD WHO WILL PROVIDE!"*

Some time later God tested Abraham. He said to him, "Abraham!" "Here I am," he replied. Then God said, "Take your son, your only son, whom you love—Isaac—and go to the region of Moriah. Sacrifice him there as a burnt offering on a mountain I will show you." Early the next morning Abraham got up and loaded his donkey. He took with him two of his servants and his son Isaac. When he had cut enough wood for the burnt offering, he set out for the place God had told him about. On the third day Abraham looked up and saw the place in the distance. He said to his servants, "Stay here with the donkey while I and the boy go over there. We will worship and then we will come back to you." Abraham took the wood for the burnt offering and placed it on his son Isaac, and he himself carried the fire and the knife. As the two of them went on together, Isaac spoke up and said to his father Abraham, "Father?" "Yes, my son?" Abraham replied. "The fire and wood are here," Isaac said, "but where is the lamb for the burnt offering?"

---

* Preached by Dr. Terry Eves at the Church of the Good Shepherd in N. Augusta, SC on July 30, 2017. Theme: God calls Abraham and us to radical faith and radical faithfulness. Jesus, the Gospel and the Kingdom that He proclaims come to us in the New Testament wrapped in Old Testament so that we can properly understand Who He is, what the Gospel is, and what He has come to do.

Abraham answered, "God himself will provide the lamb for the burnt offering, my son." And the two of them went on together.

*When they reached the place God had told him about, Abraham built an altar there and arranged the wood on it. He bound his son Isaac and laid him on the altar, on top of the wood. Then he reached out his hand and took the knife to slay his son. But the angel of the L*ORD *called out to him from heaven, "Abraham! Abraham!" "Here I am," he replied. "Do not lay a hand on the boy," he said. "Do not do anything to him. Now I know that you fear God, because you have not withheld from me your son, your only son."*

*Abraham looked up and there in a thicket he saw a ram caught by its horns. He went over and took the ram and sacrificed it as a burnt offering instead of his son. So Abraham called that place The L*ORD *Will Provide. And to this day it is said, "On the mountain of the Lord it will be provided." The angel of the L*ORD *called to Abraham from heaven a second time and said, "I swear by myself, declares the L*ORD*, that because you have done this and have not withheld your son, your only son, I will surely bless you and make your descendants as numerous as the stars in the sky and as the sand on the seashore. Your descendants will take possession of the cities of their enemies, and through your offspring all nations on earth will be blessed, because you have obeyed me." Then Abraham returned to his servants, and they set off together for Beersheba. And Abraham stayed in Beersheba.*
Genesis 22:1-19 (NIV)

Brothers and sisters, God has carefully led and graciously prepared Abraham for this crucial moment in his life. This is the tenth and last time God speaks to Abraham. After this story He will not speak again to him in Genesis. Genesis 22:1-2, *"Some time later God tested Abraham."* If we are honest with ourselves, in our non-Christian or less-than-fully redeemed Christian thoughts and emotions, we don't like this. In our secret selves we want *a God Who provides only*, not a God Who also tests. We want a God who promises and gives and redeems, not a God Who also takes and demands. Yet God is this way with His people. If we want anything else and anyone else, and seek to worship any other kind of God, then it is an imaginary God; it is an idol we have created and such an act is idolatrous and therefore dangerous!

*"Take your son, your **only** son Isaac,* whom you love *and go to the region of Moriah . . . and sacrifice him there as a burnt offering on one of the mountains I will tell you about."* This is the first mention of love in the Bible! And it is crucial that we first hear of love here, for Isaac is not only the only son of Abraham now, he is the beloved son (Genesis 12:1). This story and Genesis 12:1-3 are the bookends between which all the Abraham stories are to be read and illuminated. In Genesis 12 Abraham is told to give up his past and his present, in Genesis 22 to give up his present and his future. He is to give up the son that he has waited for his entire life! As I worked on this sermon I was struck that Abraham and Sarai in Genesis 12 are like the disciples in Mark. When Jesus called them they abandoned their lives, left everything, and followed him.

The nature of the test is this: "Does Abraham fear God for nothing?" There are many strong and intended parallels among Genesis 22 and Exodus 20:18-21 and Job 1-2, where God tests a godly person, and where the test consists of relinquishing that which is most precious as the essence of what true faith, trust, and obedience ("fearing God") involves. God tested Abraham. Here we have the purpose for the event, but remember that Abraham and Isaac don't know this even though we do. Why was Abraham tested? Because since the time of his call decades earlier, his life in Canaan has not proven his devotion to God was *unconditional.* In the earlier stories it is unclear, frequently uncertain to Abraham and Sarah whether they can count upon God and trust Him and unclear whether God can count on Abraham and his obedience. Abraham struggles for obedience in every dimension of God's promises to him but of all the promises of God the one that

Abraham has the most trouble believing is **the promise of a son**. In no other area does Abraham doubt more, in no other area does he manipulate his life and manipulate others so much to try to bring the fulfillment of the promise without trusting and obeying God. What Abraham does, when it looks like he cannot trust God to fulfill his promises to Abraham and Sarah, is choose to deal with the situation the way his Canaanite neighbor would. And now decades later it is final exam time! *The issue is whether Abraham is willing to surrender to God that which is the most precious to him.* To help you identify the significance to Abraham and part of the significance to you, ask yourself as you hear this story and sermon, what area(s) in your life with and before God have you struggled with more than any other for faith, trust, and obedience? Where would God test you if it were you and not father Abraham in this story?

What also makes this test so hard is the apparent contradiction between what God has promised and what God now commands. For Isaac is not only the only son and the beloved son, he is also the divinely chosen son who is the bearer of God's promises! "Through Isaac will your descendants be numbered . . . Isaac must be killed." The issues become very clear and very simple: 1) what does he love the most, the gifts of God or the God Who gifts? and 2) what does Abraham put his trust and hope in, the promised son or the God Who has given him the promised son? For Yahweh is the giver of life, all life belongs to Him, and what He has given He can command to be given back. God has the right to ask for Abraham's son. He has the right to ask for anything that He has given Abraham, because Isaac's life was God's gift in the first place, even though he bears **all** of Abraham's hopes for the future! Even though he is the divinely chosen son through whom alone the promises of the Covenant can be fulfilled.

"Your son, your only son, whom you love . . . and sacrifice him as a burnt offering!" Here too the narrator helps us. It is true that Yahweh has demanded the life of Abraham's son Isaac, his son, his only son, whom he loves. But it is also true that the God of Abraham has twice in these

stories saved from death the son through whom the covenant promises will not descend, the sent away son, once in chapter sixteen when Ishmael was in Hagar's womb and once more in the story that occurs immediately before this one. In chapter sixteen, after she and her preborn son have been saved from death by the sent Angel of Yahweh, Hagar is the only woman in the OT who gives God a name. And that name is "El Roi," for she said "*I have now seen the One **who sees me**!*" "That is why the well was called Be'er Lahai Roi ("*the well of the Living One Who Sees Me*"). And in chapter twenty-one, when again Hagar and Ishmael face death from thirst, God **hears** not Hagar weeping, but the boy. If God has saved the rejected son twice from looming death, then what *might* God do for the divinely chosen son, the beloved son through whom all the covenant promises will descend? We must wait and see.

Genesis 22:3, "*Early the next morning.*" I love this about Abraham!

Genesis 22:5, "*The boy and I will go and worship and the boy and I will return.*" This is amazing. Abraham now trusts God and believes that since God is faithful He must fulfill all of His promises to Abraham.

Genesis 22:7-8, "*God himself will provide the lamb my son.*"

Genesis 22:12, "*Now I know that you fear God.*" *To what extent* will Abraham obey? For the fear of God here is not a feeling or an emotion, it is wholehearted faith in God and wholehearted trust of God inseparably linked to wholehearted obedience to God! Here in this story Abraham becomes the supreme example for Israel, the one who demonstrates as a representative individual the kind of obedience to God that is to characterize Israel as a whole. This story is clearly intended to present Abraham as the model for the life of faith and the life of faithfulness. He is the model Israelite and the model Israelite worshipper. He demonstrates the response to God that should and must characterize Israel and the church as a whole. This chapter becomes the whole Abraham story in miniature. Abraham is willing to offer to Yahweh that which is dearest to him. This is why Abraham became the father of the faith. As Walter Brueggemann says so well,

"No one was promised so much, given so little, was asked for it back and still remained faithful and trusting in God than Father Abraham!"

Genesis 22:12, *"Do not lay a hand on the boy."* In Genesis 22:13, Abraham looked up and there in a thicket he saw a ram caught by his horns . . . and sacrificed it instead of his son. What an incredible act of divine providence! The God who commands Abraham to offer Isaac has also purposely, providentially, graciously provided a male ram caught in the thorns.

Genesis 22:14, *"So Abraham called the name of that place Yahweh Yireh"* ("Yahweh sees/Yahweh provides"). Now this all took place on Mount Moriah. "Moriah"—*what does Moriah mean and where is Moriah?* It means either "The Place of Seeing" or "The Place of Fearing." Moriah is mentioned in only one other place in the whole Old Testament, in II Chronicles 3:1 where we learn that Solomon builds the Temple on Mount Moriah, the place of divine choosing, the place where Abraham sacrificed, and the place where the angel of Yahweh hovers while David's sacrifice stops the death plague sweeping Jerusalem. Father Abraham offers by faith and in faithfulness the first sacrifice at the future site of the Solomonic Temple.

"As it is said to this day, 'On the mount of the Lord it shall be provided.'" The God who saw and provided for Abraham in his desperate need, the God who heard and rescued is the God who continues to see and to provide in the Temple in Zion! The God who sees, and the God who hears, is the God who will provide.

Genesis 22:15, *"Because you have done this"* all the promises of the Abraham Covenant that God gave in Genesis 12:1-2 are re-given and reconfirmed (Genesis 22:17-19). And how does God respond? The God Who tests is the God Who now abundantly provides and gives! The speech of the angel of Yahweh at the crucial moment of the sacrifice refers to the result of the test in verse 12, *"now I know that you fear God because . . . ."* Here the crucial matter is that Abraham fears God. Fear of God concerns doing rather than feeling. Here we deal with the mystery of the significant role of Gospel obedience. The covenant has now been confirmed on both sides. God therefore doubles the promise of offspring. It is therefore fitting that the Angel, for the first time in the Abraham stories, links the two earlier promises of Genesis 13:16 and 15:5: *"stars of heaven and as the sand on the seashore."* The sequence of the reality is also important. For it is only Yahweh's faithfulness to Abraham that has created Abraham's faithfulness in Yahweh.

"Because you have obeyed me," because Abraham radically believes and also radically obeys—because the Abrahamic Covenant (like the New Covenant) is bilateral, and not unilateral. This is one of the crucial places in the Abraham story that is Abraham's equivalent to God sealing the covenant with Abraham in Genesis 15. And let's never forget that God has tested Abraham in relation to the divine promises that Abraham has struggled the most to believe and to obey. Every time before this when Abraham cannot believe the divine promise of a son, he did an end run and tried to solve the problem the Ancient Near Eastern way: adoption, and when that failed, a surrogate mother.

It is only as Abraham is willing to obey this hard command that he discovers that he will not in fact lose by it, but instead will gain great blessing (Genesis 22:16-18). It is only as the initial gift is freely and obediently surrendered that Yahweh restores it again with renewed blessing. Yahweh tests Abraham to increase his obedience to Him, to draw out His people into further obedience and righteousness. All the promises of Genesis 12:1-3 are renewed (with an emphasis on off-spring). The promised son returned, the promise of offspring doubled, divine blessing, the land promise renewed, the curse function of the Abrahamic Covenant will be fulfilled, and, finally, *"all nations on earth will be blessed* [that's us here too] *because you have obeyed Me!"* Notice that by ending this story with the theme of blessing this story ends the same way that Genesis 12:1-3 ended. When we faithfully do the will of God, God provides for our other needs also.

What does it mean to take the Lord's Supper in the context of this story? I could say many things, because this story is so full of the Gospel and Gospel truths, but I will only say a few. It means to be reminded again that God in the Gospel demanded of Himself what He did not ultimately demand of Abraham. It is to be reminded that God demanded of Jesus His son what He demanded only partially of both Abraham and Isaac. That God the faithful Father, Who Himself has only one Son, the one and only Son, the Beloved Son, tested His son in the same ways and also even more severely than he tested Abraham. And Jesus shows the same wholehearted faith in God and wholehearted trust of God inseparably linked to wholehearted obedience to God that Abraham showed!

But Jesus is not only the new Abraham, He is also the new and final Isaac, the faithful son who also carries the wood of His own sacrifice up the mountain called Golgotha. There he dies as a "whole burnt offering" for Abraham and instead of, for Isaac; and instead of, for Sarah; and instead of, and for all His people; and for each of you, if you belong to Him. And Jesus is not only the new Isaac—He is the new and final Ram of God (caught in the thicket) of Whom Abraham said, *"God Himself will provide the lamb, my son."* That the God Who appears on Moriah and in Zion has fully revealed Himself now in His own Son, His one and only Son Whom He loves. And the place where father Abraham offers the first sacrifice at the future site of the Temple is the place where the Faithful Father offered the Obedient One and Only Son Whom He loves as the Final Sacrifice. That God, at the time of Abraham, provided the place for sacrifice so that to this very day, we too—this morning and every morning—can say: "On the mountain of Yahweh He has seen our need, your need . . . He has seen, He has provided." It is to understand the message of amazing grace that God has withheld nothing and given everything, and that Jesus, His one and only Son Whom He loves, has withheld nothing and believed and trusted and obeyed in everything, and gave everything, so that His enemies may become His beloved sons and daughters! We need to hear and believe these transforming words: *"God himself will provide the lamb for the burnt offering."* Or, as Psalm 103:6 puts it, *"O Israel, put your hope in the Lord, for with the Lord is unfailing love and with him is full redemption. He himself will redeem Israel from all their sins."*

Brothers and sisters, this is nothing less than the Gospel itself that this text proclaims! *"That God so loved the world, that He gave his one and only Son, that whoever believes in Him shall not perish but have everlasting life."* Come and eat, come and feast on the Lamb of God who takes away the sins of the world, come and eat the true bread sent from heaven. *"For the bread of God is he who came down from heaven and gives his life for the world!"* Because the God Who sees and the God Who hears is the God Who provides and the God who hears and sees is the God Who rescues from death!

We also need be reminded to do full justice in this text that this same God Who gives us redeeming love also comes with demands that call us to radical obedience, for this same God calls **us** to wholehearted faith in God and wholehearted trust of God inseparably linked to wholehearted obedience to God. Brothers and sisters, may the Holy Spirit so work this Gospel into our hearts and lives, into our very DNA, that in all things, small and momentous we live in such faith and trust and radical obedience that the faithful God Who comes to us with both promises and demands, says again and again in each of our stories, *"Now I know that you fear God!"* and on that first day of the complete renewal of all things may each of us hear these words "Well done, my good and faithful servant, enter into the joy of your Lord!"

PRAYER: "OH FAITHFUL AND GENEROUS Father, the Heavenly Abraham who gave Your Heavenly Isaac, Your one and only Son Whom You love, for us and instead of us, so work in us that we increasingly imitate Abraham and Jesus' radical faith and radical faithfulness, for Your glory and for our good! In Jesus' name, Amen.

"God from all eternity did, by the most wise and holy counsel of his own will, freely and unchangeably ordain whatsoever comes to pass; yet so, as thereby neither is God the author of sin, nor is violence offered to the will of the creatures, nor is the liberty or contingency of second causes taken away, but rather established."

— Westminster Confession of Faith, III.1

"ALL THINGS WORK TOGETHER FOR GOOD"*

When Joseph's brothers saw that their father was dead, they said, "It may be that Joseph will hate us and pay us back for all the evil that we did to him." So they sent a message to Joseph, saying, "Your father gave this command before he died: 'Say to Joseph, "Please forgive the transgression of your brothers and their sin, because they did evil to you."' And now, please forgive the transgression of the servants of the God of your father." Joseph wept when they spoke to him. His brothers also came and fell down before him and said, "Behold, we are your servants." But Joseph said to them, "Do not fear, for am I in the place of God? As for you, you meant evil against me, but God meant it for good, to bring it about that many people should be kept alive, as they are today. So do not fear; I will provide for you and your little ones." Thus he comforted them and spoke kindly to them. Genesis 50:15-21 (ESV)

The story of Joseph found in Genesis 37-50 is one of the most remarkable in all the Bible. It provides a perfect illustration of the truth taught to us in Romans 8:28, *"And we know that for those who love*

---

* This is a new sermon written for *Celebration* by Dr. Mark Ross. Theme: God uses the wicked deeds of sinners for the accomplishment of His saving purposes toward His people.

God all things work together for good, for those who are called according to his purpose." It demonstrates that even our most bitter sufferings work together for good under the gracious and powerful hand of God, who rules over and directs all that happens for the accomplishment of His saving purposes for His people.

Yet this passage also teaches us that seeing just what God is doing through all our sufferings is not something we can easily or quickly discern while they are occurring. We may have to wait a very long time before we can see that any good has come from them. In Joseph's case it took many long years. In other cases, it may take much longer. In some cases, we may have to wait until the eternal kingdom arrives. Even so, we have this promise from God, and the story of Joseph provides us with a powerful encouragement to trust that promise from God completely. Additionally, it anticipates for us the amazing grace of God revealed in the salvation of sinners through the redeeming work of Christ.

The story begins by telling us that Joseph was seventeen years of age (Genesis 37:2). The information that follows in Genesis 37:3-11 is background information to the tragic events that unfold in verses 12-36. Joseph was Jacob's favorite son, and that favoritism was not hidden from his brothers. Jacob made a very special robe for Joseph, usually called *"a robe of many colors,"* although the exact meaning of the Hebrew phrase is uncertain (Genesis 37:3). Whatever it was, clearly it was quite different from the robes of his brothers and it marked him out as Jacob's favorite.

This favor did not work to Joseph's advantage, for his brothers hated him because of it. Joseph added to the trouble by bringing a bad report about his brothers to his father (Genesis 37:2), and he shared too freely with them the dreams which he had of gaining superiority over his brothers, and even his parents (Genesis 37:5-11). His brothers hated him all the more for his dreams and his words. Even his father rebuked him for it, which was probably a rare event in the household of Jacob.

The enmity between Joseph and his brothers grew over the years and came to a breaking point when he was seventeen. The brothers were away from home pasturing the flocks of Jacob when Joseph came to check on them. The brothers first thought to kill him, but were dissuaded from the murderous act by Reuben, the eldest brother. They threw him into a pit while they pondered what to do. When a caravan of Ishmaelite traders passed by, Judah suggested that they sell Joseph into slavery, and then deceive Jacob about his fate by saying he had been killed by a wild animal. Thus begins the downward spiral in Joseph's life, as he is torn away from his father's love to become a slave in Egypt (Genesis 37:12-36).

Once there, Joseph was bought by an officer in Pharaoh's army, Potiphar. Joseph's fortunes began to improve somewhat, for we are told *"the LORD was with him"* (Genesis 39:2). He quickly became the chief steward in the household. But in time this situation too went bad and Joseph suffered another reversal. Potiphar's wife, having been repeatedly rejected by Joseph as she tried to seduce him, falsely accused him of assaulting her. Joseph was thrown into prison.

For some time he remained there, but there too the LORD was with him. Joseph came into favor with the keeper of the prisoner, and soon he was overseeing the other prisoners. During this time he came to know two of Pharaoh's servants who had also been thrown into the prison, the chief cupbearer and the chief baker. One night they both had dreams, and by the gift of God, Joseph interpreted the dreams, which revealed the fate of the two men. The chief cupbearer would be released from prison and be restored to his former position, while the chief baker would be executed. Things turned out just as he predicted. Joseph asked the chief cupbearer to remember him to Pharaoh when he was restored, but the chief cupbearer forgot the kindness which Joseph had shown to him. For another two years he remained in prison (Genesis 40).

Finally, one night the Pharaoh had a very troubling dream and he called for the magicians and wise men of Egypt, but none of them could interpret the dream. Then at last the cupbearer remembered Joseph and how he had been able to interpret both his dream and the chief baker's. His conscience was stricken for his failure to remember Joseph after he was restored. He spoke to Pharaoh about Joseph and confessed his fault (Genesis 41:9-13). Quickly Pharaoh called for Joseph, and he was able to interpret the dream. Pharaoh's dreams revealed that seven years of plenty were to come in Egypt, but they would be followed by seven years of famine. Joseph urged Pharaoh to take preparatory action by storing up twenty percent of their harvests so that they would have food to sustain them in the years of famine. Pharaoh considered this an excellent idea, and he appointed Joseph to be over all this work. He would be second only to Pharaoh in all the land of Egypt. The downward spiral in Joseph's life had at last been dramatically reversed, and he was now in a very favored and comfortable position in life.

The Scriptures tell us that Joseph was thirty years old when he entered the service of Pharaoh (Genesis 41:46). This means that it had been thirteen years since he was sold into slavery—thirteen years of service as a slave, and then as a prisoner, after being ripped away from his father's love because of the hatred his brothers had toward him. Through this period of time he had been a trusted, faithful, and dutiful steward in Potiphar's house, only to be dismissed under false accusations and thrown into prison. He then became a faithful and dutiful overseer in the prison, only to be forgotten by the chief cupbearer for the kindness shown to him.

Certainly, there were blessings he enjoyed across these years, for the LORD was with Joseph. He always seemed to bounce back from his setbacks. At the same time, we must not forget that he was a slave and a prisoner in a foreign land. How did he respond to these trials? What happened to his faith during this time? The narrative of his life moves along with only an outward description of his circumstances, without ever telling us about his inward response to his sufferings. But after his elevation to Pharaoh's right hand, we are given a brief mention of his family life that throws a little light upon the inner life of Joseph during this time.

Joseph was a given a wife by Pharaoh when he entered his service, and during the years of plenty which followed two sons were born to him (Genesis 42:45-52). It is in the names of the two children that we gain a little light on Joseph's inner struggles of faith, and perhaps on how he survived the thirteen years of severe trials. The first is called Manasseh, for Joseph said, *"God has made me forget all my hardship and all my father's house."* If the simple straightforward narrative of Joseph's life left us with the impression that he simply soldiered on and never really felt the pain of all that he suffered, "Manasseh" lets us know that Joseph struggled the way any of us would. It was only as things began to work out for Joseph in a better way that he could look back and say that God had helped him move on. With the birth of his second son, Ephraim, he could also see that God had made him fruitful. He now had much for which to be thankful. He still could not see the reasons behind all that he had suffered, but he could at least look forward with a measure of hope, believing that God had not forgotten him after all. God had made him forget, and God had made him fruitful. Somehow his faith had survived during these trying years, and now he was able to trace the hand of God's sustaining grace and favor in his life. But there was a much greater discovery for him yet to make.

As God had revealed to Joseph, the seven years of plenty were followed by the years of famine. As food grew scarce across the Middle East, no doubt there were many from foreign lands who came to Egypt as word spread that grain could be found there. Then one day visitors arrived from the land of Canaan, the land of Joseph's birth. They too were seeking to buy grain, in hopes that they could sustain their families through the famine. Joseph's very own brothers now stood before him. While they did not recognize Joseph, he immediately recognized them. It would be some time before Joseph made himself known to them, and in the intervening time he would be testing them in various ways. Three full chapters of the story unfold before

Joseph reveals himself to them (Genesis 42-44). During this time Joseph remembered his childhood dreams (Genesis 42:9), and saw that in them God had been revealing the future. Their fulfillment was now at hand. More than that, however, Joseph came to see the reason behind all that he had suffered, and how God had sent him ahead of the brothers to Egypt, where he would rise to power and be in a position to save his family from perishing in the years of famine (Genesis 45:5). God had indeed worked all things together for good.

As we ponder this remarkable story of God's providence, let us consider three lessons that stand out prominently before us in the final words that Joseph speaks, the words of our text (Genesis 50:15-21). First, let us consider **the evil that was done to Joseph**. They had planned to kill Joseph, but finally settled upon selling him into slavery, and deceiving their father about what they had done and what had happened to Joseph. Effectively, twenty-two years of Joseph's life with his own family had been taken from him, counting the thirteen years that had passed from the time he had been sold into slavery, the seven years of plenty that followed, and then the two years that the famine had been in the land when Joseph's brothers came to Egypt (Genesis 45:6). Joseph's brothers were responsible for all the pain and suffering he endured during those years, as well as the grief and sorrow they caused Jacob with the loss of his favorite son. They had meant to do evil against Joseph (Genesis 50:20), and they had done evil against him. God had indeed brought good out of it all, but what they had done was evil nonetheless. God's mysterious providence had worked in and through their evil deeds and worked salvation through them, but the good result which had come from their evil deeds did not make those deeds any less evil.

Joseph's brothers knew that they had done evil. Across the years, the guilt of their crime stayed with them. When they stood before Joseph in Egypt, though as yet they did not know that it was he, their consciences seized them when he accused them of being spies—*"In truth we are guilty concerning our brother, in that we saw the distress of his*

soul, when he begged us and we did not listen" (Genesis 42:21). These words
tell us just how frightful it all had been for Joseph. The look on his
face had never left their minds. Truly, they had done evil, and they
knew it. In our text they confess *"the evil that we did to him"* (Genesis
50:15), and they sought forgiveness for their transgression and their sin
(Genesis 50:17). What they had done, they had done freely, and the full
responsibility for it was on their shoulders. Nothing could excuse their
guilt. Their only hope was for the forgiveness of their sin.

There is a second lesson for us in this passage: **God meant all
this for good**—*"As for you, you meant evil against me, but God meant it
for good, to bring it about that many people should be kept alive, as they
are today"* (Genesis 50: 20). God was also at work in all the events that
took Joseph to Egypt, and with all that happened to him there. The
point is not merely that God used these things for good, but that He
meant them for good. God did not simply react to the evil which was
done, and then turn it toward a good outcome; God meant for it all to
happen. It had all occurred according to His plan. Just as fully as the
brothers plotted and schemed as they meant to do evil against Joseph,
so God had planned and appointed these events to occur. He was
working in and through the evil intentions of the brothers, though
His intentions were for good, to bring it about that the children of
Israel should be kept alive through the years of famine—*"God meant
it for good, to bring it about that many people should be kept alive, as they
are today"* (Genesis 50:20).

We see in the Joseph narrative the great mystery which unites
divine sovereignty with human freedom and responsibility. The
first, we might say, interpenetrates the second, without destroying it.
The second remains what it is: human beings acting freely, without
compulsion, doing as they choose to do, being fully responsible for
what they do. Even so, God is at work in their choices, ordaining
their choices, for the accomplishment of His own holy purposes. The
mysterious union of these two has been beautifully expressed in the
Westminster Confession of Faith—"God from all eternity did, by the

most wise and holy counsel of His own will, freely and unchangeably ordain whatsoever comes to pass; yet so, as thereby neither is God the author of sin, nor is violence offered to the will of the creatures, nor is the liberty or contingency of second causes taken away, but rather established" (WCF III.1).

This statement does not resolve the mystery we have before us; it only states it. We are not brought closer to understanding *how* all this can be true; we are only assured that it is. Many proof texts from the Holy Scriptures are supplied in the confession to support the doctrine, giving further confirmation to what this one passage tells us—*"As for you, you meant evil against me, but God meant it for good."* What Joseph's brothers meant for evil, God meant for good. The same events were expressive of their evil intentions and His holy intentions.

We see this elsewhere in the Holy Scriptures. Isaiah points to the evil deeds done by the Assyrians when they conquered the northern kingdom of Israel and threatened the southern kingdom of Judah. The Assyrian king came with evil intent—*"it is in his heart to destroy and to cut off nations not a few"* (Isaiah 10:7). He came with bravado—*"shall I not do to Jerusalem and her idols as I have done to Samaria and her images"* (Isaiah 10:11). He came with pride and arrogance—*"By the strength of my hand I have done it, and by my wisdom, for I have understanding"* (Isaiah 10:13). Yet God was also determining these events for his own holy and just purposes, for he says—*"Ah, Assyria, the rod of my anger; the staff in their hands is my fury. Against a godless nation I send him, and against the people of my wrath I command him, to take spoil and seize plunder, and to tread them down like the mire of the streets"* (Isaiah 10:5-6). Assyria was nothing but the axe in God's hand (Isaiah 10:15). Yet, what Assyria did was evil nonetheless, and the day would come when *"the Lord had finished all his work on Mount Zion and on Jerusalem"* and he would *"punish the speech of the arrogant heart of the king of Assyria and the boastful look of his eyes"* (Isaiah 10:12). Divine sovereignty and human responsibility united in the same events.

This brings us to a third observation we should make from this text: **the revealed purpose of God to work salvation for His people**—*"to bring it about that many people should be kept alive, as they are today"* (Genesis 50:20). Through all the evil deeds of Joseph's brothers, through the decision of the Ishmaelites to sell Joseph in Egypt, through his purchase by Potiphar and the favor Joseph secured in his house, through the wicked solicitations of Potiphar's wife, through her false accusations and Joseph's subsequent imprisonment, through the interpretations given to Joseph for the dreams of the chief cupbearer and the chief baker of Pharaoh, and finally through the interpretation given for the dreams of Pharaoh, God was acting for the deliverance of His people. Through all these things Joseph was sent before his brothers to Egypt, where he was elevated to a position second only to the Pharaoh, so that all the grain of Egypt would be at his disposal, to keep his people alive. Joseph had earlier made this point when he revealed himself to his brothers, for by then he had come to understand the divine purpose at work in all the tragic events of his life—*"God sent me before you to preserve life"* (Genesis 45:5).

It is a marvel of the working of God's grace that Joseph can so freely and fully forgive his brothers for the evil that they had done to him and for all the subsequent sufferings they caused. Yet grace was given to Joseph to forgive them, for God had yet a further purpose for this whole story of rejection, suffering, and finally deliverance and elevation for Jacob's son. It was for revealing the work of salvation to be accomplished through God's Son. For like Joseph, Jesus would also be rejected and delivered over to the Gentiles by His people. Like Joseph, Jesus too would later be found alive by His people, and be raised to a position of authority and power, having been raised from the dead and seated at the right hand of God. Like Joseph, Jesus too would be willing to forgive the evil that had been done to Him. Like Joseph, Jesus too would open the storehouses of God to save many people from death, making atonement through the blood of His cross. Like Joseph, Jesus too would deal graciously toward those who had done evil against Him, and promise to provide for them and for their little ones (Genesis 50:21).

Like Joseph, Jesus was a man *"despised and rejected of men, a man of sorrows and acquainted with grief"* (Isaiah 53:3). *"But he was wounded for our transgressions; he was crushed for our iniquities; upon him was the chastisement that brought us peace, and with his stripes we are healed"* (Isaiah 53:5). *"Yet it was the will of the LORD to crush him; he has put him to grief; when his soul makes an offering for guilt, he shall see his offspring; he shall prolong his days; the will of the LORD shall prosper in his hand"* (Isaiah 53:10).

Truly, God works all things together for good for those who love God, for those who are called according to His purpose (Romans 8:28). He has the whole world in His hands, the evil and the good. He orders them all for the accomplishment of His purposes, and His purposes consummate in the salvation of His people. Surely then we can trust such a sovereign and gracious God, whatever the sufferings of our days might be, however long they must be borne, however strange and inexplicable they might seem. Others may mean evil against us, and they might do evil against us. But God means it for good, for those who love God, for those who are called according to His purpose. His sovereign purpose is to keep us alive, delivering us from sin and death, forever and forever. Thanks be to God.

PRAYER: GRANT, ALMIGHTY FATHER, THAT we may so trust in You that we will see Your hand in all of life, in the evil and the good, and trust that when others do evil against us, You mean it all for good. In your perfect timing, we ask you to deliver us from evil, establish us on the Solid Rock, and bring us at last to dwell with You forever. In Jesus' name we pray, Amen.

"Let us practice the fine art of making every work a priestly ministration. Let us believe that God is in all our simple deeds and learn to find Him there."

—A. W. Tozer

"ANSWERING THE CALL OF GOD"*

Now Moses kept the flock of Jethro his father in law, the priest of Midian: and he led the flock to the backside of the desert, and came to the mountain of God, even to Horeb. And the angel of the LORD appeared unto him in a flame of fire out of the midst of a bush: and he looked, and, behold, the bush burned with fire, and the bush was not consumed. And Moses said, I will now turn aside, and see this great sight, why the bush is not burnt. And when the LORD saw that he turned aside to see, God called unto him out of the midst of the bush, and said, Moses, Moses. And he said, Here am I. And he said, Draw not nigh hither: put off thy shoes from off thy feet, for the place whereon thou standest is holy ground. Moreover he said, I am the God of thy father, the God of Abraham, the God of Isaac, and the God of Jacob. And Moses hid his face; for he was afraid to look upon God. And the LORD said, I have surely seen the affliction of my people which are in Egypt, and have heard their cry by reason of their taskmasters; for I know their sorrows; And I am come down to deliver them out of the hand of the Egyptians, and to bring them up out of that land unto a good land and a large, unto a land flowing with milk and honey; unto the place of the Canaanites, and the Hittites, and the Amorites, and the Perizzites, and the Hivites, and

---

* Preached by Dr. Toney Parks at First Presbyterian Church, Augusta, GA on January 4, 2015. Theme: God is calling your name; your time, gifts, and talents are to be used by God to minister to the needs of others.

the Jebusites. Now therefore, behold, the cry of the children of Israel is come unto me: and I have also seen the oppression wherewith the Egyptians oppress them. Come now therefore, and I will send thee unto Pharaoh, that thou mayest bring forth my people the children of Israel out of Egypt. And Moses said unto God, Who am I, that I should go unto Pharaoh, and that I should bring forth the children of Israel out of Egypt? And he said, Certainly I will be with thee; and this shall be a token unto thee, that I have sent thee: When thou hast brought forth the people out of Egypt, ye shall serve God upon this mountain. Exodus 3:1-12 (KJV)

There is a spiritual song among members of the African American Church; the title is "Hush, Somebody's Calling My Name." It is believed that God was calling the one singing to prepare for deliverance, to be freed from whatever the bondage might have been. This was a call to hope, and to believe that God would provide and deliver those singing out of bondage. We find ourselves hearing the same lyrics today, still asking ourselves the question asked by the hymnist, "what shall I do?" The writer hears what sounds like Jesus calling his name. There is a continuous voice calling his name. Once again, the hymnist asks the question, "what shall I do, what shall I do?" The hymnist resounds, "soon one morning death come creeping in my room. Oh, my Lord, what shall I do?" The writer seemed joyful and glad that he had gotten his religion on time; he was glad that the trouble he was experiencing would not last always; with jubilation, he asks the question again, "what shall I do, what shall I do?" God is calling you to answer His call to service.

As we consider our society, we know that there are individuals, knowledgeable and skilled in various careers, employed by companies and corporations throughout this state. They have been called, employed, or hired to make a productive contribution to the well-being of the organization for which they are employed. God has spiritually equipped us, as members of the Body of Christ, for the work of service or ministry. Every member of the Body has been equipped and called by

God to make a spiritual contribution to the Church. God has equipped and called you; you are expected to answer.

I answered the call of God. Even in my early experiences, I was being equipped; I was being prepared. I had a very eventful childhood. I lost my mother, a single parent, while still in elementary school. Having to face the trials and tragedies of life, God summoned me at a very early age. I heard the call of God on my life. The call came to me through the Word of God, which I heard taught in Sunday school and preached at worship services. I responded to the invitation given by the pastor. I trusted and believed in the promises of God. I believed that He would protect and provide for me, just as He did for the children of Israel. God is calling you to step out on faith. You are being called today to trust the God of Abraham, Isaac, and Jacob. God is calling you to use the gifts given to you in your mother's womb. God is calling you. You are being called to share your gifts with others. God wants to work through you. Hush! Can you hear Him calling you through His Word?

God demonstrated a deep concern and passion for the well-being of His people. God watched and listened to the plight of His people. He recognized their sorrow, pain, and affliction. God was listening to their needs. He listened to their cries, just as He listens to our prayers. Because of His sovereign nature, He knows. He is our *"very present help in times of trouble"* (Psalm 46).

God gets our attention: God speaks to us in ways which no one else is able to do, only Him. In the text, God gets Moses alone as he leads the flock to the far side of the wilderness. This is where Moses meets God alone; he came to the Mount of God. God gets Moses' undivided attention. God uses the power of nature, sickness, disaster, and calamities to get the attention of those He seeks. It is not until God gets our attention that we decide to listen to Him. Life has a way of taking our focus away from God. We become so busy with the affairs and activities of life that worship and ministry become secondary.

Moses saw that the bush was on fire, but noticed it was not consumed. God had Moses' attention. Moses sought an explanation. God used the burning bush as an opportunity to speak into the life of Moses. God gets our attention so that He can carry out His perfect will through us. I invite you to think of a time when God has spoken to you through another person, through a miracle, or through a situation that could not be explained. God uses situations and people in our lives to lead us in the right direction. We are led by the preaching, teaching, and testimony of others each and every day. Your attentiveness and your willingness to listen to the Word of God presents the opportunity for you to answer Him.

God makes Himself known. God wants you to know He is present: *"And when the LORD saw that he turned aside to see, God called unto him out of the midst of the bush, and said, 'Moses, Moses.' And he said, 'Here am I'"* (Exodus 3:4). Moses took the time to hear God. There comes a time in life when a person needs a personal relationship with God and knows He really is in their life. Moses listened to God and got to know Him for himself. God's call is a personal call; God called Moses by name. There is nothing about you that God doesn't know. God is constantly calling and seeking to bring His people to a closer relationship. When God calls, we must always respond positively to God's call: Moses said *"Here am I."* Likewise, we should respond with, "Here am I, Lord."

We must obey God. We are called to go and do exactly what God has told us to do. God is Holy; we are called away from our sinful past. We are called to separate ourselves for the purpose of being used by God. God tells Moses exactly who He is: *"I am the God of your father, the God of Abraham, the God of Isaac, and the God of Jacob"* (Exodus 3:6). God is God of the **promise**. He is God of the **covenant**. What God has done for others, He will also do for you.

God calls us to service. God calls because there is a need to serve. He is calling because He wants you to serve. When He calls, He expects an answer. He expects us to respond in a positive way. God tells Moses, *"I will send you to Pharaoh that you may bring my people, the children of Israel, out of Egypt"* (Exodus 3:10). God knows that Moses is the right man for the job, in spite of his weaknesses, fears, and past failures. God knew

Moses was equipped to do the job. Likewise, He knows you and that you're equipped for the job to which He is calling you.

God had anointed, appointed, and prepared Moses for this mission. God knows us better than we know ourselves. He knows what we can and cannot do. If God leads you to do something, He will always enable you to accomplish it. God is calling us, because He is concerned about the suffering of His people. God is calling us, because He has seen the affliction and misery of His people. God is calling us, because He has heard the cries of His people. God sees the oppression; He sees the affliction; He sees the suffering; He sees the pain; He sees the injustice. God comes to rescue His people. God comes to meet their needs. God promised that He would always be with us.

Answer the Call of God. God is calling you. God seeks your attention, in spite of all that you have been through. He has spared you for His purpose. The Lord is calling you today. He is telling you to . . .

- Tell them that the Lord sent you. Tell Pharaoh to let my people go!

- Abraham said, here I am, send Me! Samuel said, here I am, send Me!

- Jeremiah said, here I am, send Me! Paul said, here I am, send Me!

Can you hear the Lord calling you today? I invite you to answer the call of God. God wants to do something through you. God will not call you for a task that He will not prepare you to accomplish.

PRAYER: MOST GRACIOUS FATHER, WE thank You for the opportunity to be part of the Body of Christ. We realize the importance of using our gifts for the edifying of the Church. We pray that You will give us the courage and the wisdom to lead our families, our communities, and our churches out of the hands of the enemy. We pray for our leaders, politicians, and most of all our families. Please hear our prayer. Lead us through the challenges and trials of this life. We praise and honor You in the precious name of Jesus Christ, Amen.

"This is, indeed, God's story, the story of his unfathomable love and grace, his mercy and forgiveness. And He means for it to become our story, too . . . "

—Gordon Fee

"GOD'S PROVIDENCE: MOSES AND THE EXODUS"*

And the Lord said, I have surely seen the affliction of my people which are in Egypt, and have heard their cry by reason of their taskmasters; for I know their sorrows; And I am come down to deliver them out of the hand of the Egyptians, and to bring them up out of that land unto a good land and a large, unto a land flowing with milk and honey . . . Exodus 3:7-8a (KJV)

Friends, I am grateful for this opportunity to say a few words about God's mercy and His providence as we find them in The Book of Exodus.

No human being can defeat the will of God. Pharaoh did his best to defeat the will of God. He was the most powerful man on earth at that time, but all his efforts to thwart the will of God came to nothing. Pharaoh ordered the midwives of Egypt to kill all the male children born into Hebrew families. To be sure, the midwives feared this powerful tyrant, but they quietly refused to obey him. Why? Because they feared God more. So Moses survived as an infant, in spite of Pharaoh's plan. God was watching over him.

His family hid him in the rushes of the Nile River, in a basket made of reeds, and that is where the daughter of Pharaoh found him one

---

* Preached by Mr. Fred Guyette in Bowie Chapel at Erskine Theological Seminary in spring 1997. Theme: No human being can defeat the will of God. Exodus shows us that Moses had a teachable heart, but Pharaoh did not.

day. She brought Moses into Pharaoh's house. What were the odds of that happening, humanly speaking? As he grew up, he was educated by the best teachers. His benefactors thought he was destined to be a high-ranking official in Egypt. But Moses had loyalties they did know about, and his education was not yet complete. Every day Moses was becoming more aware of a harsh reality: Egypt's economy depended on the oppression of Hebrew slaves. God kept on speaking to Moses' conscience about this, and a deep desire to change Egyptian society began to grow in his heart. There came a day when he witnessed an Egyptian overseer mistreating one of the Hebrews, and in his anger, he rose up and killed the Egyptian.

So Moses became a fugitive. He himself did not know where he was going. Yet God was leading Moses, even in his fear and desperation, to the place and the purpose He had appointed for him. Moses kept moving, so as not to be captured by Pharaoh's men, and eventually he came to Midian. Now Moses was exhausted from his journey, and thirsty, too. His heart must have leapt up when he saw that he was coming to a well. But as he got closer, he saw that some men were harassing a group of young women who were just trying to draw water for their sheep. So Moses came to the aid of the young women. We might be tempted to think that this was just a random event, something that happens every day, but we do well to remember: God is present in even the smallest encounters we have with people, just like He was in this one at the well. Moses asked nothing of the women in return, he did not even introduce himself, but that is how he met Zipporah, and her father, Jethro. Eventually Moses and Zipporah were married. He learned how to tend sheep there in Midian, what it takes to care for a flock, little knowing that he would be able to put those skills to use in a different context later on, when God called on him to do something much more important.[1] All during these years, says Calvin:

> *Moses had to live in the open air, and to bear heat, and cold, and hunger, constant fatigue, the care of cattle, and other troubles. God, indeed, miraculously supported the holy man in the performance*

*of his arduous duties; **but still the internal conflict must have gone on,—why does God so long delay and suspend what he so long ago determined?** It was, then, no ordinary virtue which overcame these distracting assaults, which were constantly renewing his anxiety; whilst, in the meantime, he was living poorly, in huts and sheds, as well as often wandering over rough and desert places . . . .*[2]

After many years out there in the desert, God spoke to Moses again, this time through the Burning Bush. God called him by name, *"Moses."* And Moses responded, *"Here I am."* This answer shows that Moses had a teachable heart and that he was ready to obey.[3] And what did the Lord reveal to Moses? He said: *"I am the God of your fathers, Abraham, Isaac, and Jacob."* With these words, God showed the continuity of His purpose. He had been shaping events long before Moses arrived on the scene. It was at the Burning Bush that Moses began to see how God is the Lord of the past, the present, and the future, because He said: *"I **have heard the cry** of My people, I **am come down to deliver them**, and I **will lead them** to a land flowing with milk and honey"* (Exodus 3:7-8).

Moreover, it was at this point that Moses began to see more clearly what God's plan for the Hebrews might be. He told Moses to return to Egypt, to march straight into Pharaoh's court, and deliver a message from God: "Let My people go!" We should not let this point escape our attention: None of this was Moses' own idea. He did not think he was the right person for this mission, but Moses somehow knew better than to resist The Master of the Universe. Moses did not yet know what the endgame would be—how Pharaoh would react, or what God might do subsequently. All he knew on that day was that he was being summoned to take the next step, to go and deliver God's message to Pharaoh.

In obedience to God's call, Moses entered Pharaoh's court and delivered the message. But listen now to Pharaoh's response: *"Who is the Lord that I should obey his voice to let Israel go? I know not the Lord, neither will I let Israel go"* (Exodus 5:2).[4] Such fateful words! If only Pharaoh had listened to Moses! But soon enough, Pharaoh would become better acquainted with the Lord, when God sent ten plagues upon Egypt:

1. The rivers of Egypt turned to blood. All the fish died, too, and for a whole week the people could not drink the water.
2. A Plague of Frogs—the din of their croaking filled the air.
3. Flies covered the land—neither man nor beast could draw a breath.
4. A Plague of Wild Animals harassed the Egyptians, frightening everyone in their path.
5. Pestilence killed the farm animals of the Egyptians.
6. A Plague of Boils afflicted the people of Egypt.
7. A Hail Storm came and destroyed many of Egypt's crops.
8. A Plague of Locusts came and ate whatever crops were left.
9. And that was followed by a Plague of Darkness, during which the Egyptians were terrified and would not even venture out of their homes.

But Pharaoh still refused to acknowledge that God is sovereign over all. Time and again, Pharaoh said *"No!"* to God. And, finally, God sent the most terrible plague of all: The Angel of Death came and killed every firstborn son among the Egyptians. So that is what it took to persuade Pharaoh that he should not ignore the Word of the Lord. After those devastating losses, all the Egyptians were overcome with grief. Pharaoh quickly did an about-face and told Moses to leave Egypt without delay. So the Hebrews left Egypt, without even waiting for that day's bread to rise, which is why the celebration of that day came to be known as The Feast of Unleavened Bread.

But then Pharaoh did something almost incomprehensible. He changed his mind *again* and sent his chariots after the Hebrews, hoping to capture them and bring them back into the house of bondage. When the Hebrews saw that they were in danger of being trapped with their backs to the sea, they almost gave up hope. Then suddenly the unexpected happened—God parted the Red Sea and allowed them to cross over to the other shore. Thinking that they could make it too, the Egyptians continued in hot pursuit. But the waters flooded back in over them, and their chariots were inundated. That is why The Song of Miriam says, *"the horse and rider he has thrown into the sea!"* (Exodus 15:21).

Now, Beloved—this is just one of the stories of God's providence. The Bible tells us much more about God's eternal purposes, and how He wants us all to grow in faith, hope, and love for Him and for each other. It is Israel's story, yes, but it can become our story too, whenever we recite the mighty acts of God and tell others how He rescued the Hebrews from slavery, *"with a mighty hand and an outstretched arm"* (Deuteronomy 26:8).[5] It becomes our story when we turn to Him with teachable hearts and renew our covenant with God, just as God's people did many years later in the Book of Nehemiah.[6]

PRAYER: GRANT, ALMIGHTY GOD, THAT since Thou daily invitest us to Thyself with so much kindness and benevolence, and since Thy word continually sounds in our ears,—O grant, that we may not become deaf through the depravity of our flesh, but be attentive to hear the doctrine of salvation, and become so teachable and obedient, that we may be willing to be turned wherever Thou pleasest, and to be guided in the way Thou pointest out to us, until we shall at length reach that blessed rest, which has been prepared for us in heaven by Jesus Christ our Lord. — Amen.[7]

"You frequently say in class that the same Scripture text can be preached in many situations and different circumstances. I want you to come to my church and preach Exodus 4:24-26 for Mother's Day."

—John Paul Marr

"THANK GOD FOR FAITHFUL CHRISTIAN WOMEN WHO SERVE A FAITHFUL GOD!"*

Now the LORD had said to Moses in Midian, "Go back to Egypt, for all those who wanted to kill you are dead." So Moses took his wife and sons, put them on a donkey and started back to Egypt. And he took the staff of God in his hand. The LORD said to Moses, "When you return to Egypt, see that you perform before Pharaoh all the wonders I have given you the power to do. But I will harden his heart so that he will not let the people go. Then say to Pharaoh, 'This is what the LORD says: Israel is my firstborn son, and I told you, "Let my son go, so he may worship me." But you refused to let him go; so I will kill your firstborn son.'"

At a lodging place on the way, the LORD met him and was about to kill him. But Zipporah took a flint knife, cut off her son's foreskin and touched his feet with it. "Surely you are a bridegroom of blood to me," she said. So the LORD let him alone. (At that time she said "bridegroom of blood," referring to circumcision.) Exodus 4:24-26 (NIV)

---

* Preached by Dr. Terry Eves at Troy ARP Church, Troy, SC on Mother's Day, May 12, 2013. Theme: God calls us not just to Gospel faith but also to faithfulness and Gospel obedience in all things and in all circumstances, even strange ones.

In II Timothy 3:16-17, Paul tells Timothy: *"All Scripture is God-breathed and is useful for teaching, rebuking, correcting and training in righteousness, so that the man of God may be thoroughly equipped for every good work."* It is one thing to believe this theoretically, but it is another thing altogether to believe it and trust in its truth when the minister, the session, and the church are committed to expository preaching, faithfully preaching through all of Scripture and not just picking and choosing. Wise ministers, sessions, and churches want this because they have come to understand that "it takes a whole Bible to make a whole Christian" man, woman, boy, and girl.[8] Thank God that this church is committed to this. It is a joy for me to preach in a church like this with your commitments. It is in faithful commitments like this that we really come to more clearly understand the life-changing truth of texts like these. Week after week we learn to trust God's provision to feed His people with His good Word, nurture our faith, and grow us in Gospel obedience when we are committed to preach and teach every text in their sequence in Scripture. Have you ever read a passage in Scripture that the first or even third time you read it seems to say little or nothing beneficial to you? Or that troubled you at first and you secretly wished it really weren't there? Well, ministers can have these moments too! What do I do on Monday morning in my office when the next text that comes up in the Bible to preach from seems to have nothing to say to us, at least nothing that seems edifying or uplifting? Do I truly trust God to feed his flock with *"every word that proceeds from God's mouth?"* Do I truly believe that the Bible's promises about itself are really true, or are these naïve hopes that have to be abandoned in the cold hard reality of Gospel ministry as we come to understand that **only some** Scripture is inspired and useful?

Brothers and sisters, I struggled with these questions in my first years in Gospel ministry in the church, seeking to faithfully preach texts to feed God's hungry people that seemed at first to have no good Gospel food in them at all. But time and time again the Holy Spirit taught me that what looked like no food or poor food for God's hungry people had much higher nutritional content than I first thought. Let me share such a text with you this morning, namely Exodus 4:24-26. I could have given this sermon several different titles, but I decided to name it, "Thank God for Faithful Christian Women Who Serve a Faithful God!" But men, please don't tune me out because there is much here to teach Christian men as well.

What should we do when we encounter strange, or disturbing, or difficult texts, or texts that seem to have nothing in them to teach us or reshape us? Let me suggest that we do two things. First, pray for the Spirit to teach us. Then we should ask four questions. 1) What is the rest of this chapter talking about? 2) Does the text I'm reading now remind me of anything God said earlier in the Bible? 3) Does God say anything in the rest of this book I am reading that is intended to help me with this text? 4) Does God use this text anywhere later in the Bible to help me see additional truths and meanings for my life?

How does the rest of this part of the chapter help me out? Well, brothers and sisters, it helps us so much that I will only be able to briefly point out a few of the helps that they provide. Let's read it in the context of the previous paragraph. Please open your Bible again and read the verses just before ours (read Exodus 4:21-23). Notice that our text is so closely tied *to* the previous paragraph that in the Hebrew text it doesn't even identify the person God is seeking to kill other than say *"him ... him ... his foreskin ... touched his feet with it ... so the Lord left him alone."* Who is God trying to kill here? Well the same God who has been talking about the death of firstborn sons in Egypt is now seeking to kill another firstborn son. Is Moses a firstborn son? No, Aaron is his older brother. Then who is God seeking to kill? Moses' firstborn son, Gershom. But why is God trying to kill him?

Does the text I'm reading now remind me of anything God said earlier in the Bible? Yes. To better understand why God is trying to kill Moses' son, we need to see how crucial a role God's covenant with Abraham is in Exodus, in the Sinai Covenant, and in one of the signs of the Sinai Covenant. We must also better understand the significance of the covenant sign of circumcision in Genesis 17. Let's go back and hear a verse or two in Genesis 17:9-14 from the promise giving and command giving God, especially verses 12 and 14: *"for the generations to come . . . every male . . . must be circumcised . . ."* and *"any uncircumcised male who has not been circumcised in the flesh, will be cut off from his people,* **he** *has broken my covenant."* Moses himself is woefully negligent here in both the past and in the present. In Moses' commission with God's call to him out of the burning bush in Exodus 3-4, God gives him a sign in Exodus 3:12 that all of Israel will worship the God who reveals Himself in fire at Mount Sinai.

God calls Moses to be the one through whom He will deliver, consecrate and enter into a new covenant with His people, and Moses has not consecrated his own two sons to the Lord of the Covenant! But the God of Abraham takes the promises and commands of the Abrahamic Covenant and the sign of the Abrahamic Covenant far more seriously than Moses does! God knows and wants us to know that the Gospel and the covenant and the signs of the covenant are a two-edged sword, and that covenant privilege results in both grace and obligation! And notice what the Lord of the Abrahamic and soon to be Lord of the Sinai Covenant does. Since Moses has not cut off his son's foreskin, God now seeks to cut off Gershom from the covenant people, just as He instructed father Abraham in Genesis 17. God is doing nothing here that is inconsistent with His grace, His promises, or His commands.

Notice too, Moses' sad, unfaithful consistency here! Moses who passively did nothing before or after the burning bush to put the divinely commanded sign of the covenant on his children, apparently stands here passively while God seeks to kill his firstborn son! **But, fortunately, Moses has a wife!** To better understand the significance of what Zipporah is doing here, let's now ask question three. Does God say anything in the rest of this book I am reading that is intended to help me with this text? Yes, Zipporah here stands in relation to a theme that is quite prominent in Exodus 1-15. Pharaoh's monstrous, murderous plan was frustrated again and again. His wrath and anger was faced and resisted by brave women. Zipporah faithfully and obediently stands in the proud and life-changing company of the two Hebrew midwives, Shiphrah and Puah, Moses' brave mother's and sister's resistance to Pharaoh's policy of genocide, and Pharaoh's daughter who will adopt Moses as her own son! Zipporah stands in continuity with impressive company indeed. She knows what to do, she does it, and again Hebrew children are saved from death!

How else does what God says in the rest of Exodus help me understand and obey this text? Let's think again about what is happening here—because Moses has not obeyed God's clear command, God now seeks to kill his firstborn son. Zipporah decisively acts and obeys God's clear command. When God sees the blood as a visible sign that He has been obeyed, He ceases to attempt to kill Gershom and departs. Does this remind you of anything later in Exodus? YES! Brothers and sisters, do you see what is going on here? God does for Gershom here **what He will soon do for all Israel!** This story is preparation for and dress rehearsal for Passover night when Yahweh will stalk the entire land of Egypt and kill the firstborn son of any family, Egyptian or Israelite, who has not obeyed His word. Whenever He walks by a house that does not have the blood of the Passover sacrifice visible on the doorpost and lintel, He comes into that house and kills the firstborn son. Do you remember that the only requirement for participation in the meal is to be circumcised? Having the sign of the Abrahamic Covenant on you is the only formal requirement to join the people of God in eating the covenant meal, one of the signs of the Sinai Covenant, and experience covenant blessing instead of cursing, covenant life instead of covenant death. Earlier in Exodus faithful women braved the wrath of Pharaoh to save newborn Israelite boys, but Zipporah goes beyond them all. Faithful, obedient Zipporah now braves the wrath of God Himself to save her and Moses' firstborn son from death! Thank God for faithful, brave, Christian women.

Why does God choose goodness and mercy rather than wrath and judgment for Gershom? Now we must also ask question four—does

God use this text anywhere later in the Bible to help me see additional truths and meanings for my life?! How does reading this Exodus text in the context of the whole Bible help us? How does reading it in the context and content and the Gospel light of all of the other texts in the whole canon help us? Well, there is one more great Gospel truth that we need to hear and obey here. When we read this story in the light of the rest of the Bible, then we come to better understand that God no more ultimately wills the death of Gershom in Exodus 4 than he willed the death of Isaac in Genesis 22 or the death of Moses in Exodus 32-34 where the guiltless Moses offers his own life for the sinful, total rebellion of all of Israel in the sin of the Golden Calf.

Brothers and sisters, **please listen to my words, for this story articulates the heart of the Gospel itself**! God does not will the death of Isaac, or Gershom, or Moses because He has willed the death of His one and only Son, Whom He loves, to save us from our sins. He wills the death of His, not just firstborn Son, but His only Son Whom He loves, Who will die on the cross in John's Gospel at the very time that the priests and Levites are sacrificing the Sinai Covenant lambs to fulfill Passover law. He wills the death of the only fully faithful Israelite and human being who had ever lived! He wills the death of the only fully faithful Mediator of the New Covenant who like Moses offers His innocent life as Mediator for a guilty people and, this time, God says YES, rather than no! Yes, the New Covenant (even Greater than Moses) Mediator dies **instead of** Isaac, **instead of** Gershom, **instead of** Moses. Because of God's great love for His people in the Gospel, Christ dies for the guilty, He dies **for** Isaac and **for** Abraham, **for** Gershom and **for** Moses, **for** Zipporah, **and for each of us if we have entered into Jesus' Kingdom**. Have you entered into this Kingdom, or if you have not, will you enter this Kingdom of Light and Life and Peace today? Embrace this Gospel freely offered to you, free because it has been paid by Jesus and opened up to you by Jesus! If you are in His Kingdom, then seek to become more like brave Zipporah in her wholehearted service to the faithful God and Lord!

PRAYER: LORD OF THE COVENANT, Who is rich in mercy and in grace, work Your good Gospel deeper and deeper in our hearts and lives. May we join faithful Zipporah in seeking Your Kingdom and Your good will in all things. In Jesus' name, Amen.

"When a preacher speaks as a herald, he must cry out 'the word.' Anything less cannot legitimately pass for Christian preaching."

—Haddon W. Robinson

"PIN THE 'TALE' ON THE DONKEY"*

"Do you believe in talking snakes?" So the question asked me during the floor exam of Second Presbytery of the Associate Reformed Presbyterian Church.

At the time, I, a candidate undergoing the process of licensure, did not realize that the teaching elder's question was referring to an inquiry Karl Barth underwent decades ago in an attempt to understand and discern his approach and his handling of God's Word. Amid my own challenging oral exam, I just did not appreciate how my "talking snakes" questioner actually was trying to learn if any Barthian or neo-orthodox leanings had crept into my doctrine of the Word. I am blessed to say that my education at Erskine Theological Seminary, under God's providential care, has only strengthened my appreciation and admiration of the Bible as God's Word.

Perhaps on the floor exam that day I should have played it safe and cited the *Westminster Confession of Faith*, chapter five, paragraph one, where God upholds, directs, disposes, and governs all creatures, from the greatest to the least. Yet when that teaching elder asked me, "Do you believe in talking snakes?" I responded, with a sarcastic smile,

---

*   This sermon was scheduled to be preached by the Reverend John Paul Marr at the General Synod of the Associate Reformed Presbyterian Church, meeting at Bonclarken Conference Center in June 2016. The early conclusion of synod prevented the presentation of the sermon. Theme: As prophets of the Most High God, ministers must preach God's Word in His will and way of love.

looking at him directly, saying, "I do believe in talking donkeys . . . , sir."
Obviously, my rebuttal referenced the following passage of Scripture.

> *But God was very angry when Balaam went, and the angel of the*
> *Lord stood in the road to oppose him. Balaam was riding on his*
> *donkey, and his two servants were with him. When the donkey saw*
> *the angel of the Lord standing in the road with a drawn sword in*
> *his hand, she turned off the road into a field. Balaam beat her to*
> *get her back on the road.*
>
> *Then the angel of the Lord stood in a narrow path between the*
> *vineyards, with a wall on either side. When the donkey saw the*
> *angel of the Lord she pushed against the wall and pressed Balaam's*
> *foot against the wall. So he struck her again.*
>
> *Then the angel of the Lord went ahead and stood in a narrow place,*
> *where there was no way to turn, either to the right or to the left.*
> *When the donkey saw the angel of the Lord, she lay down under*
> *Balaam. Balaam's anger was kindled, and he struck the donkey*
> *with his staff.*
>
> *Then the Lord opened the mouth of the donkey, and she said to*
> *Balaam, "What have I done to you, that you have struck me these*
> *three times?"*
>
> *Balaam said to the donkey, "Because you have made a fool of me.*
> *I wish I had a sword in my hand, for then I would kill you."*
>
> *The donkey said to Balaam, "Am I not your own donkey, which you*
> *have always ridden, to this day? Have I been in the habit of doing*
> *this to you?" "No," he said.*
>
> *Then the Lord opened the eyes of Balaam, and he saw the angel*
> *of the Lord standing in his way, with his drawn sword in his hand.*
> *Balaam bowed down and fell on his face. The angel of the Lord*
> *said to him, "Why have you struck your donkey these three times?*

Behold, I have come to oppose you because your way is perverse before me. The donkey saw me and turned aside before me these three times. If she had not turned aside from me, surely just now, I would have killed you and let her live."

Then Balaam said to the angel of the LORD, "I have sinned, for I did not know that you stood in the road against me. Now therefore if it is evil in your sight, I will turn back."

The angel of the LORD said to Balaam, "Go with the Moabite men, but speak only the word that I tell you." So Balaam went on with the princes of Balak. Numbers 22:22-35 (NIV)

This section of the larger Balaam narrative in Numbers chapter twenty-two could be summarized as a story of two donkeys. We all are familiar with this Sunday school story of Balaam and his talking donkey. It is set within the larger context of the book of Numbers where God continues revealing His holy and merciful character and His redemptive intent for humanity through His chosen people. This Balaam and his donkey segment is not some mere legendary account, inserted later and used for didactic purposes—only to teach and model, in a supposedly fable-like manner, the powerlessness of enemies to hinder Israel achieving God's purpose for them. This is also not simply an inspirational devotion to show how God can act on behalf of His people despite their recurring failures to follow Him faithfully. This wonderful donkey tale, pun intended, has grammatical features of a straight-forward historical narrative, yet also artistically contains poetic elements, solid storytelling techniques that make it memorable and meaningful for us as ministers of God's Word.

Consider the threefold patterns in the passage, developing with increasing intensity and humor: three times the angel of Yahweh blocks the way; three times Balaam does not perceive the danger ahead; three times the donkey does see and responds, saving Balaam's life; three times Balaam responds, beating the donkey and ultimately desiring to kill the donkey. Yes, there is comedy in the telling, but there are also consequences in what is being told. The indicting irony of this story forces us to ask a question: which one, Balaam or the donkey, is oblivious and truly obstinate to God's will and way? Which one is the real donkey?

Obviously the first "donkey" *is* the donkey. When God wants to announce great themes, influence multitudes, change lives, shape destinies, He does so through whoever and whatever He wishes: you, me, even a donkey. This is an act of the Almighty Creator God breaking the boundaries of biology and physiology. Here our donkey, a creature sometimes viewed as superficially stupid and stubborn, is more perceptive than the professional seer. The author heightens the contrast further by having the female donkey see divine matters more clearly than this practiced male diviner.

Therefore, the second and greater "donkey" . . . is Balaam. Balaam is an oxymoron, maybe more of a **moron** in this episode of his life than he realizes. Balaam travels about cursing military enemies for money, a mercenary fortune-teller, a hired-gun soothsayer, a weather forecaster concerned more about ratings than predicting the rain. Balaam is so self-absorbed in this passage and therefore so easily tempted to assimilate to the will and the way of the world. Balaam is a most unexpected spokesman for God, chosen to bestow blessings upon God's people, with the world watching, with the world in fact witnessing God's gracious faithfulness to His people. Balaam moves from being a magical specialist of some worldly repute into functioning as a prophet of the Most High God, Yahweh the Redeemer. Balaam is that oxymoron, a mixture of God's grace and the depths of human sin, just like you and me, especially each time we get behind a pulpit to preach Christ and Him crucified, for there we desperately need God's grace to rightly handle God's Word. We need the conviction and gospel mercy of His Word upon us before it can be communicated through us. Perhaps we all should acknowledge how we all are just one small step away from being Balaam.

Look at how our Scripture passage begins on a strange jarring note, a startling eruption of God's anger kindled against an apparently, what we think at first, obedient Balaam. *"Go on your way,"* God has told Balaam in verse twenty, yet then God gets angry that Balaam goes. You and I as elders have often been placed in this Balaam predicament so that God can search out our hearts, test and know our anxious thoughts, and see if there is any offensive way in us. On the surface Balaam appears to be doing God's will, but by the end of the passage we know Balaam is going *on*, but he is not going *in* God's way. Instead Balaam has rushed recklessly in his own way. The passage begins with God's anger, but throughout the passage we subsequently see Balaam's anger actively kindled against a donkey that at its own cost seeks to protect its master.

Now, Balaam had imagined he was to go about this God-ordained contract prophecy in his own fashion. Therefore, he needs to undergo a conviction by the Word of the Lord. God orchestrates this, exposing Balaam's self-oriented preaching, by opening the mouth of the donkey. And then God opens Balaam's eyes. Finally, at the end of the passage, Balaam sees the danger, the angel, standing there as an adversary, the text tells us, opposing Balaam's perverse way.

The angel repeats the donkey's question. Balaam confesses, *"I have sinned."* Balaam admits his willful transgression, recognizing his utter "missing" of the right way, the God way, he must go. Balaam acknowledges both his sinful actions and the deeper sinful attitude that erupted in his own brutish, beastly behavior. By God's grace, Balaam is set back on the proper path of going in the will and way of the Lord, turning from the world of his sponsor, the king of Moab, to the true authority of the Word of the Lord. Four times in chapter twenty-two Balaam has stated that he could only speak that which Yahweh puts in his mouth: verse 8, verse 19, verse 35, and verse 38. It takes all four times to get God's message out of Balaam's mouth.

Balaam is not intended to be an example to follow, but a warning to heed. He may acknowledge his sinning, but never acknowledges a need for a Savior to save him from his sin. Peter in his second letter to Christians in the region known as Asia Minor warns the church of infiltrating false teachers, who, like the false prophets of old, have left the straight way and wandered off to follow the way of Balaam, son of Beor. Peter describes Balaam as one who loved the wages of wickedness. Peter then relates how Balaam was rebuked by a donkey—a beast without speech—who spoke with a man's voice and had restrained the prophet's madness.

Balaam's madness may have been restrained, but the rest of his story continues only a few chapters later in the Book of Numbers. For the Lord commanded Moses and the Israelites to take vengeance upon the Midianites who had treated them as enemies at Peor, seducing the Israelites into sexual immorality and worshipping the Baal of Peor. So, the Israelites fought against Midian, killing the five kings of Midian as well as Balaam son of Beor. The Scriptures tell us Balaam was killed with the sword—reminding us of the angel of the Lord with a drawn sword, who had barred Balaam's path from walking outside of God's will and way.

The angel of the Lord with a drawn sword will again appear in the history of Israel: he appears to Joshua; he appears to King David. In the New Testament, the Gospel writer Luke will look to Numbers chapter twenty-two as he relates the conversion story of his companion Paul. In Acts chapter nine, Paul, in Balaam-like fashion goes in his own way thinking he is doing God's will, breathing out murderous threats against the Lord's disciples. This time it is not the angel of the Lord with a drawn sword; it is the Risen Lord. The Resurrected Jesus will ask Paul a more penetrating question than the donkey had asked Balaam: *"Why are you persecuting me?"* Then the Risen Jesus will open the eyes of Paul and put words in Paul's mouth—the gospel—just as the Risen Jesus has done for each one of us. Yes, we are constantly tempted to repeat the sin of Balaam. And yes, God has given us the gospel to live and to proclaim. No longer is there an angel of the Lord wielding a drawn sword before us, now there is a wooden cross before us, the powerful expression of God's will and His way of whom we, you and I, are messengers. We are angels of the Lord wielding the Word of God, sharper than any two-edged sword.

Now there is the Risen Savior who, by the Holy Spirit, puts His words into our hearts and then, coming out of our mouths, words to bless His people, blessing them with the gospel, not for profit or prosperity, not for our own peace or pleasure, not for our own purity and prestige. We speak the truth of God's Word in His will, in His way, in His love. We preach Christ and Him crucified because that is the message God has given to this lost and losing world. That is the message each one of us needs—facing our own sins and trusting the work of the Savior for our salvation. Every one of us must honestly respond to whether we believe, not just in talking snakes, but in the good news of Jesus Christ. Rather than a talking donkey challenging our willfulness and waywardness, we are confronted daily (if not hourly) by the cross of Christ and asked: what are we going to do with the Word of truth it speaks?

Maybe we in the Associate Reformed Presbyterian Church need to remember our roots and get going with the free offer of that gospel. Maybe we need to get our "donkeys" in gear and get going in our calling of God's will and God's way, speaking the truth in love to a world that is moving more and more antithetical to the will and way of God. Maybe, dare I say it, we need to get off our backsliding messages, which promote a Balaam self-love and personal gain and glory, and again commit to our roles as true prophets of the Redeeming Yahweh, proclaiming for God's glory His sacrificial love in Christ Jesus. Let us reaffirm here, in our day, to bless God's people with the great reality and powerful Word of the gospel.

PRAYER: SEARCH US, O GOD, and know our hearts; test us and know our anxious thoughts. See if there is any offensive way in us, and lead us in the way everlasting. In Jesus' name, Amen.

"I think this is going to be the most religious century, ever."

—Doug Culver[9]

"ABIMELECH . . . AND SACRED HISTORY"*

And he went to his father's house at Ophrah and killed his brothers the sons of Jerubbaal, seventy men, on one stone. But Jotham the youngest son of Jerubbaal was left, for he hid himself. And all the leaders of Shechem came together, and all Beth-millo, and they went and made Abimelech king, by the oak of the pillar at Shechem. When it was told to Jotham, he went and stood on top of Mount Gerizim and cried aloud and said to them, "Listen to me, you leaders of Shechem, that God may listen to you." Judges 9:5-7 (ESV)

"If you then have acted in good faith and integrity with Jerubbaal and with his house this day, then rejoice in Abimelech, and let him also rejoice in you. But if not, let fire come out from Abimelech and devour the leaders of Shechem and Beth-millo; and let fire come out from the leaders of Shechem and from Beth-millo and devour Abimelech." And Jotham ran away and fled and went to Beer and lived there, because of Abimelech his brother. Abimelech ruled over Israel three years. Judges 9:19-22 (ESV)

Abimelech and the company that was with him rushed forward and stood at the entrance of the gate of the city, while the two companies rushed upon all who were in the field and killed them. And Abimelech fought against the city all that day. He captured the

---

* Preached by Dr. George Schwab at Warrington Presbyterian Church in Abbeville, SC on August 14, 2016. Theme: Divine Providence is invisible to us—but working nevertheless.

*city and killed the people who were in it, and he razed the city and
sowed it with salt. When all the leaders of the Tower of Shechem
heard of it, they entered the stronghold of the house of El-berith.
Abimelech was told that all the leaders of the Tower of Shechem
were gathered together. And Abimelech went up to Mount Zalmon,
he and all the people who were with him. And Abimelech took an
axe in his hand and cut down a bundle of brushwood and took it
up and laid it on his shoulder. And he said to the men who were
with him, "What you have seen me do, hurry and do as I have
done." So every one of the people cut down his bundle and following
Abimelech put it against the stronghold, and they set the stronghold
on fire over them, so that all the people of the Tower of Shechem
also died, about 1,000 men and women. Then Abimelech went to
Thebez and encamped against Thebez and captured it. But there
was a strong tower within the city, and all the men and women and
all the leaders of the city fled to it and shut themselves in, and they
went up to the roof of the tower. And Abimelech came to the tower
and fought against it and drew near to the door of the tower to
burn it with fire. And a certain woman threw an upper millstone
on Abimelech's head and crushed his skull.*   Judges 9:44-53 (ESV)

*Thus God returned the evil of Abimelech, which he committed
against his father in killing his seventy brothers. And God also
made all the evil of the men of Shechem return on their heads,
and upon them came the curse of Jotham the son of Jerubbaal.*
Judges 9:56-57 (ESV)

Are you ever tempted to doubt that God is at work in the world?
Doesn't it seem that things are proceeding in the wrong way? If God
really were governing events, why is the church on the wane in her
traditional lands? Isn't the history of the world just what the news
media says it is—nothing but politics and economics? Is that all there
is? Why are secular humanism and Islam winning out against the

Gospel? Chapter nine of Judges offers a perspective on world events and how to regard them.

The chapter is about Gideon's two sons, Jotham and Abimelech. Abimelech wanted to be king. He wanted that very badly. He took money from a shrine of Baal, hired some thugs, and with them killed all of Gideon's other sons—except Jotham, who fled. Jotham then stood on the mountain top, and prophetically declared judgment upon Abimelech for what he had done, and on the city of Shechem for putting him in power. He said in effect, "Let fire break out and consume those who put him in power! Let Abimelech answer for his deeds!" After pronouncing the curse, Jotham fled.

So, except for that one speech, Jotham really doesn't do anything. Abimelech drives the action through the rest of the long chapter.

And boy, is there a lot of action! Mostly it is about Abimelech or his political supporters behaving badly. The city of Shechem put him in power, and almost immediately, bad blood develops between them. Shechem has buyer's remorse, and there's a humorous line in Judges 9:27, where it says that they *"ate and drank and cursed Abimelech."* Everyone involved with this atrocious story were opportunists who conceptualized kingship as a power grab, without any regard for the people, for justice, or for God. One man named Gaal in Shechem mouthed off against Abimelech and then tried to lead an army against him.

The text describes how Gaal looked out of the city gate in the early morning before it was light, and at the base of the mountain thought he could see men approaching. They seemed to appear out of thin air, like ghosts (sorry, this doesn't come through in our English translations; see Judges 9:37).

These ghostly men, appearing out of the mist like wraiths, were Abimelech's forces, coming to take the city. There was a battle, Abimelech ransacked Shechem, and burned its citizens alive who had fled to a tower for refuge. Abimelech had no compassion at all; he was some sort of psychopath, reveling in suffering and death. *He burned alive the very people who had put him in power in the first place!* Shechem created a monster and paid for it. But the monster was still at large in the story.

Having successfully ruined Shechem, Abimelech decided to continue his reign of terror by laying siege to city after city throughout Israel. He became worse than any foreign oppressor had been. He set his sights on the nearby city of Thebez. He ransacked that town as well, and again the people fled for refuge to a tower. Abimelech was in the process of setting fire to that tower too, when a woman threw a millstone down from the tower, which hit him on the head and cracked his skull, resulting in his death. Good riddance! His troops then dispersed and went home, ending his oppression as quickly as it had begun.

Well, that is basically chapter nine of Judges. But there are two concluding verses at the end of the chapter that help give it perspective. *"Thus God requited the crime of Abimelech, which he committed against his father in killing his seventy brothers; and God also made all the wickedness of the men of Shechem fall back upon their heads, and upon them came the curse of Jotham"* (Judges 9:56-7). I don't know about you but that changes everything for me. What these two verses at the end of the chapter do, is surprise the reader with a perspective that is at odds with the whole tenor of the story. Remember what I said a minute ago, that after saying his piece, Jotham leaves the story, and all the action is driven by Abimelech? Not so, says these last two verses! All along, it was Jotham's curse that was driving events to their inevitable conclusion. In fact, embedded in the story, are many clues, hints as to where the story is headed, as if to underscore that the end was preordained and inevitable. The clues are the many times the word "head" occurs. In English, it says "top" of the mountains—literally it is "head." The "companies" of men are again, literally, "heads." Every time a mountain or a company is mentioned, it foreshadows Abimelech's head being smashed! He killed his brothers on one stone—and one woman killed him with a stone. Poetic justice! A righteous curse, spoken by a prophet of God, drove events until divine justice is served, and all are paid in full for the suffering they inflicted.

I said that the concluding verses contradicted the tenor of the story. This is what I mean: The story itself reads like a secular history. God is absent. It's about opportunistic would-be tyrants and political positioning. It's about mass murder and thugs doing what they can get away with. It's about people behaving badly. Secular. Not having to do with God. This is the tenor of the story.

But in the end, the veil is pulled back, and what is revealed is that, all along, events were moving forward according to spiritual principles and God's design! Simply put, Israel is just not allowed to have a secular history! Even this sordid tale is religious in character, and events are driven, in this case, by a curse against evil.

This, of course, is a paradigm on how to read *all* sacred history. It would be wrong to approach any biblical historical narrative as simply a military or political history. Israel doesn't get to have a merely political or military history.

Now, here is the punchline. Israel doesn't get to have a secular history, and neither does New Israel, the Church. You and I don't get to have things happen "just because." If we are in Christ, He works out His purposes through and in us. And everything that happens in your life, although it may seem unconnected with anything spiritual, is actually religious, through and through. If you get a flat tire, for example, it is a spiritual issue. Will you rage against God for the inconvenience? What does it take for you to misbehave?

Jesus said that if you hate in your heart, you are guilty of murder before God. We have never done the monstrous things that Abimelech did, right? Right! But, on the level of the heart's attitude, on the level of *motivation*, are there similarities between you and him? Abimelech insisted on having his own way, and when he was crossed, he did all he could to let everyone know his displeasure.

If we all agree that Abimelech was a monster, what does this say about us, when we insist on having *our* own way? How do *you* look when he is held up as a mirror on your life?

Do you have to get in the last word? Do you have to win the argument? When your personal pride has been offended, how do you behave? What does it take to strip away the outer veneer of Christian serenity and godliness and reveal the prideful heart within?

Show me what provokes you to anger, and I will have a good handle on where you and Abimelech are alike. You know the adage, "absolute power corrupts absolutely." When the restrictions of society are removed, an ordinary person is free to give full reign to his prideful heart. We see what this looked like in Abimelech's case. Have you ever treated others poorly when you had opportunity? Have you thrown temper tantrums when you didn't get your own way? When have you treated others badly?

What is your attitude when you do routine things such as the dishes? What is your motivation when you plan a vacation? How do you respond to setbacks and obstacles?

How you respond to suffering also reveals whether you truly believe that God is with you in the suffering. Or, do you believe, like an atheist, that God has nothing to do with the pain? I could belabor this point—and maybe I should—but instead, I am going to make another big theological point from Judges chapter nine. And that is this: the world, whether they know it or not, does not get to have a secular history, either. This reminds us that world events are religious, and always have been, and are moving in accordance with God's will, despite how secular things look at any given moment.

Abimelech, and his followers, and Shechem, **did not realize that events were proceeding because they were all operating under a curse and without God's blessing**. Is this not true of the age we live in today? People everywhere are going about their business unaware that a curse is hanging over them. Unaware that God will requite evil back on their heads. Unaware that they will suffer the fate of the citizens of Shechem, who took refuge in that which could not save, and perished in fire.

Jotham, whose name means "Yahweh is perfect," warned them. He said that they would be judged according to their works. And they ignored this warning, and went blithely on, to their destruction. Part of the job of an Evangelist—which all of you are—is to warn the world of the curse they are under. Peter said, *"Save yourselves from this perverse generation!"* (Acts 2:40).

Let me ask you a question. Why is chapter nine in the book? How does it move the narrative of Judges forward? There's not even a judge in chapter nine! What is it *doing* there? This is what I think: King Saul died fighting the Philistines, and this left a power vacuum in Israel. Some supported his son Ish-bosheth as the next king, and some supported David. One of the reasons the book of Judges was written was to argue that Israel should give their support to David and not to Ish-bosheth. Abimelech represented everything that was bad about Saul's administration. Its thesis is that David will not be a king like Abimelech. David will be a king with God's blessing, not a curse.

He will act justly and with compassion on his people, not like Abimelech. Part of the argument of Judges is that Israel needed a covenant-keeping king like David.

You might be aware that in the Old Testament, whenever David does something, or something is said about him, the New Testament considers that also to be true of David's son, the Messiah. For example, in the Greek wording of II Samuel 22:3, David says about God, *"I will put my trust in him."* This is exactly quoted in Hebrews 2:13, where the author attributes it to Jesus! If David said it, Jesus said it. Jesus owns everything that is David's.

What then can we make of the fact that our text ultimately commends David as king? If it commends David, it commends Jesus. It argues that Jesus is **not** a king like Abimelech, and **is** the king we need.

Jesus has everything Abimelech ever wanted. *"All authority in heaven and on earth"* (Matthew 28:19) belongs to Jesus. And what sort of King is

He? He is the sort of king that will not *"break a bruised reed, nor quench a flickering candle"* (Matthew 12:20).

He will treat you gently, when you are bruised, and not kick you when you are down. In fact, He was bruised for us (Isaiah 53:5). He is like Jotham, calling out to all who will hear, that all who listen to Him, and take His gospel to heart, will escape the curse. But the way He accomplishes this is to have the curse fall on His head instead of on yours.

Well, what will it be, brothers and sisters? Will you believe that events move themselves forward without God, and things in your life from the little to the large are more or less random? Will you live your life as a proud person, motivated by the desire to see yourself promoted, and letting everyone know when you've been crossed? Living to get even, to balance the score? Will you proceed ignoring the curse that dogs you all your days, until, in the end, it catches up with you?

Or, will you believe Jotham the Evangelist and take the warning to heart, have David's Son as your king, Who will bear the curse for you so that you can live as a citizen of His kingdom, doing the works He has called you to do? Whichever choice you make is spiritual. The one choice you don't get is to have a secular life without any ultimate connection to God.

> **PRAYER: HEAVENLY FATHER, WE PRAY** that the spiritual realities governing our lives would be ever clearer to us as we study Your Word, pray, and seek Your Face. Forgive us for faithlessly regarding both our own lives and the whole world as moving forward apart from You. Forgive us those times when we willfully sin, pretending You aren't looking, and for a moment, wishing for a secular existence. Thank You for our King, Jesus, who is everything Israel ever hoped for, and Who has secured for us deliverance from the curse. We look forward to meeting Him face to face, when He comes again as the great Judge. Amen.

"I see, gods, that you are stricken with fear of the messengers of Sea, the mission of Judge River."

—Baal

"AXE AND YOU SHALL RECEIVE"*

Now the sons of the prophets said to Elisha, "See, the place where we dwell under your charge is too small for us. Let us go to the Jordan and each of us get there a log, and let us make a place for us to dwell there." And he answered, "Go." Then one of them said, "Be pleased to go with your servants." And he answered, "I will go." So he went with them. And when they came to the Jordan, they cut down trees. But as one was felling a log, his axe head fell into the water; and he cried out, "Alas, my master! It was borrowed." Then the man of God said, "Where did it fall?" When he showed him the place, he cut off a stick, and threw it in there, and made the iron float. And he said, "Take it up." So he reached out his hand and took it. II Kings 6:1-7 (ESV)

When we read this passage, we look at the events that are recorded here, and we ask: What was the significance of this in the days of Elisha? It seems pretty trivial. In fact, it seems so trivial that critics dismiss it—Elisha just put a stick in the water and fished out the axe head! In order to understand why this has been preserved for us, we have to ask what it would have meant in the days of Elisha, the time when Baal worship was officially sanctioned, all of Israel had turned to Baal: the people of Yahweh had become the people of Baal.

---

* Preached by Dr. George Schwab at Greenville Presbyterian Church in Donalds, SC on March 19, 2017. Theme: God builds His kingdom, come what may!

We now know an awful lot about what Baal worship was, and what people believed who served him. Baal was the storm god, wielding thunder from on high, bringing rain and cloud. Think of Zeus, or Jupiter. He brought life to the earth. In the myth, when Baal died the whole earth dried up and become sterile. He made the land fertile.

Baal had some enemies. You know the saying, the enemy of my enemy is my friend; think of these enemies as being in league against him. One of these enemies is death, *Mot*, who wanted to swallow him up, and one time did, leaving Baal utterly helpless. He was dead, and there was no defeating death. Baal was swallowed up. Without intervention from other gods, he would've stayed dead forever. Another enemy was *Yamm*, the sea—a very powerful god over whom Baal could not have triumphed without help from other gods. *Yamm* had a number of titles, one of which was Judge *Nahar*, meaning Judge River, and that is the aspect of *Yamm* that is seen in our story. Because in this story, the river gets aggressive against the people of God, as in the Baal myth, the river had striven with Baal.

Here in our story, the river challenges the prophet of Yahweh and tries to harm the faithful people of God. They called themselves *"the sons of the prophets,"* a little community of those in Israel who remained faithful to Yahweh, while the rest of Israel went off to worship this mythological deity, Baal.

Judge River, in the Baal epic, went to war against Baal, and only with help could Baal defeat him. In II Kings, *Yamm* stretches out his hand to harm the people of God, wresting from them an important tool, which they were using to extend their territory. The people of God are always expanding, the gospel is always being preached, the church is always growing and multiplying, just as the Israelites multiplied in the land of Egypt that so concerned Pharaoh. In order for the sons of the prophets, the faithful remnant of Israel at that time, in order for them to expand, they needed more space. So, they're chopping down trees, taking from the banks of the river what they need to grow and fulfill God's purposes.

This is similar to a Church building project, where we take from the Bank of Greenwood or the Bank of America to grow; the sons of the prophets under the guidance of Elisha were taking from the bank of the Jordan! This appropriating needed material from the bank, this defoliating of the river, was offensive to Judge *Nahar*. The river didn't like it one bit. In this story it's as if the river has a personality. It's personified in that it does not like the sons of the prophets growing and expanding at its expense. And at the first opportunity, it grabs hold of something needed by God's people, and won't let go.

The river doesn't like its territory being encroached upon. Now, in the days of Elisha, everyone understood about Judge Nahar. All the Baal worshipers believed that Yamm was a formidable opponent who threatened to swallow up Baal. And *Mot* **did** swallow up Baal. And yet here, in this story, we see that not only can the river not stand up against Yahweh who is more powerful than Baal, but Yahweh doesn't even reduce Himself to coming down and taking issue with the river directly. Yahweh simply sends His human prophet, Elisha, to deal with the situation. See, *Yamm* can't even stand up against the prophet of Yahweh, let alone against Yahweh Himself. And in the myth of Baal, Baal was held helpless in death. But here in this story, the all-powerful and mighty *Yamm* can't even keep hold of an axe head, but is forced to yield it up.

I don't know exactly what the significance is that Elisha threw a "stick" into the water. The word for "stick" in Hebrew is the same word as the trees that were being cut down. Perhaps Elisha threw a *tree* into the water. This strikes me as a *dominion* thing—it might be that the contest is about who would have dominion here. As if *Yamm* said, "I'm going to take away your power of deforesting me," and Elisha replies, "Not only can I denude you, but I can build right into the river if I want. We can build a dock here; we can dam you if it serves our purposes!" Something like that is going on I think; some power play, a contest of who is more powerful.

And *Yamm*, the river, yields up the iron, showing that the prophet of Yahweh is more powerful against the river than Baal ever was. *Yamm* is totally intimidated by Elisha, and gives up. I think that's how the story would've been understood in the original setting, in the days of Elisha.

But this story was interwoven with other stories during the exile, in the books of I and II Kings, to meet the needs of the Jewish people captive in Babylon. What would this have meant at that time? Well, Judah had been swallowed up by Babylon, hadn't it? The waters of Babylon had engulfed Judah—they were that axe head. Did they sink down into the river, never to be seen again? Will they be captives forever? No! The promise is: if we look to the prophet of the Lord, listen to his words, if we consider ourselves to also be the sons of the prophets, those who believe what the prophets have said (like Jeremiah who said the captivity would last seventy years), then we also, like that lump of iron, will flow (the word in Hebrew is that the iron flowed like a fluid), then we also will flow right out on that promise.

We Jewish exiles are the iron whom the river desires, but we have the promise of release. When the river that swallowed us up is confronted with Elisha's tree, it must yield us up. The gods of Babylon won't hold on to us any more than *Yamm* did to that axe head. This story is the promise of our restoration. This is what the story might have meant during the exile, to those who preserved it and incorporated it into II Kings. It is a promise that God will providentially restore the people to the land, to a state of beatitude.

You know, Jesus came a number of centuries later. And when you look at His life, and His death, and His resurrection, we now are able, starting with Him, to look back at the Old Testament, and to see new meaning in all of these things, to see a meaning there that relates to Him, that we never would've guessed before He came. Jesus was swallowed up in death. Not like Baal in a mythological sense, but really as a man, He really did *die*, and really was buried. And yet, death could not hold Him. *Mot* had no sting, had no claim on Him—and thus He rose again.

It's very interesting to me, this detail of the tree cast in the water forcing *Yamm* to relinquish his hold. In the gospel, the tree is the instrument of Jesus' death. And yet His death was so unjust—because He had done nothing wrong—that death could not hold Him. I can't help it, I know it is totality transfer, but I see in Elisha's tree a type of the cross of Jesus. In His death on the cross He stripped and disarmed the principalities and powers, and the grave was forced to surrender Him—Jesus is the iron that rose again!

And of course, in the New Testament, we have the promise that as it was with that iron, and as it was with Israel in Babylon, and as it was with Christ in the grave, so it is with us. We are promised that when we die, because of the cross, death will be unable to hold on to us and we will also emerge. The book of Revelation says that someday, the sea (*Yamm*) will give up the dead in it. Death and Hades (*Mot*) will give up the dead in them, and we will all live again. That is how this passage points to the eschaton, points to the final dispensation of all things.

But I think the story also has relevance for us today. We are told that gates of hell cannot prevail against the Church. We also are living and ministering in an idolatrous culture like Elisha was; we also are sons and daughters of the prophets, a small community of faith, seeking to stay true to our God while the world is going after idols. And as we evangelize, and church plant, and grow, and expand, Satan does not like it, because every single convert we make comes out of his kingdom. We are defoliating him, we are taking from the banks of Satan.

Jesus said, *"You must bind the strong man before you plunder his house."* Satan does not like having his house plundered, any more than the river liked being stripped and bared. And so Satan strikes out against us, the devil throws up obstacles, tries to take what we need, gives us setbacks, brings persecutions—steals our axe heads. Yet if we stay true to the prophet of the Lord, stay true to Jesus, we know that whatever Satan tries to take, he will be forced to give up, because the gates of hell cannot prevail against the Church.

The river will not prevail against the sons of the prophets, and no matter what obstacle you face—and you will—you will have your axe head swallowed, and it will be expensive, but whatever he tries to do, however he tries to hinder us, he will be unable to do so. This is the promise that we find in this passage as we continue to work and grow and expand, and Satan does everything he can, but he won't be able to prevent the Church advancing until the day comes when Jesus returns and the sea and the grave give up the dead in them.

It is on that day that Jesus returns that we will in fact know the final meaning of this passage, but until then we can experience the passage's promise of God's providential care, as we in hope and faith deal with the obstacles that are thrown at us.

Amen!

PRAYER: O LORD, GRANT THAT we will have the courage to stand as sons of the prophets, the faith to believe as Elisha, and grant us the victory through Your Son, Our Lord Jesus Christ.

"'Daughter,' said the Hermit, 'I have now lived a hundred and nine winters in this world and have never yet met any such thing as Luck. There is something about all this that I do not understand: but if ever we need to know it, you may be sure that we shall.'"

—The Hermit of the Southern March, from *The Horse and His Boy* by C. S. Lewis

"ALL THE GREAT THINGS"*

Now Elisha had said to the woman whose son he had restored to life, "Arise, and depart with your household, and sojourn wherever you can, for the LORD has called for a famine, and it will come upon the land for seven years." So the woman arose and did according to the word of the man of God. She went with her household and sojourned in the land of the Philistines seven years. And at the end of the seven years, when the woman returned from the land of the Philistines, she went to appeal to the king for her house and her land. Now the king was talking with Gehazi the servant of the man of God, saying, "Tell me all the great things that Elisha has done." And while he was telling the king how Elisha had restored the dead to life, behold, the woman whose son he had restored to life appealed to the king for her house and her land. And Gehazi said, "My lord, O king, here is the woman, and here is her son whom Elisha restored to life." And when the king asked the woman, she told him. So the king appointed an official for her, saying, "Restore

---

* Preached by Dr. Max Rogland at Trinity Presbyterian Church in Rochester, MN on November 5, 2006. Theme: The Lord providentially arranges all of our life circumstances, including our conversations, to advance the work of His kingdom.

*all that was hers, together with all the produce of the fields from
the day that she left the land until now."* II Kings 8:1-6 (ESV)

I know a woman whose conversion to Christianity was triggered
by a conversation she had with a stranger on a bus. She was in a very
discouraged and depressed frame of mind. Somehow, she fell to talking with the person riding next to her, who could sense how low her
spirits were. When it came time to leave, the person got up, but before
exiting the bus simply looked at the woman and said, "When all else
fails, try Jesus."

Those words hung with the young woman, and not long afterwards
she came to admit that all else had indeed failed, and she began to
explore Christianity. She "tried Jesus" and found that He was the
solution to her struggles. All because of a conversation with a seemingly
"random" stranger on a bus!

Just consider the different factors involved in that conversation.
Consider all of the different things that had to come together perfectly
for such a result. Imagine if this young woman had been ten minutes
late and caught a different bus. She would have been surrounded by
a completely different set of people, who perhaps wouldn't have tried
to engage her in conversation at all. Or consider the physical, spatial
factors involved: What if she had been on the same bus, but sat in a
different seat? Or what if that other person had missed the bus for
some reason. Just the right set of circumstances had to come together
for these two people to have the conversation that they did, which
subsequently led to this young woman realizing that her life was
beyond her ability to fix it and that she needed Jesus.

It's what we could call a "providential conversation." The theological concept of providence is that God orchestrates the ordinary things
of life—all situations, all circumstances—to achieve His purposes for
the world. Even the things we human beings do of our own volition
(our own will), even the things we do which are opposed to God's
purpose—even those things He is able somehow to take into account
and still accomplish what He wants to accomplish.

That day on the bus, the Lord had perfectly orchestrated all of the factors involved: Who was going to be on the bus, when they were going to get on it, where they were going sit, and so on. He had orchestrated it all perfectly, so that at just the right moment, that one person could say to that young woman, "When all else fails, try Jesus."

It was a "providential conversation"—it occurred at just the right time and place for God to use in drawing that young woman to Himself. He used it for a very definite, clear purpose in His plan for that young woman's life.

In II Kings 8 we have another example of what is very much a "providential conversation." We have here the reappearance of Gehazi, last seen in II Kings 5, now speaking with the king of Israel. The king says to Gehazi, *"Tell me all the great things that Elisha has done."* That's an invitation for us as well as the king to think back over the whole narrative up to this point and to recall the many miracles performed by Elisha so far.

It's remarkable to see the king so interested in Elisha's ministry, since he has also demonstrated many times just how shallow and superficial his allegiance to the Lord is. But in any event, he asks Gehazi to tell him about Elisha's miraculous deeds, and Gehazi obliges. Perhaps he went all the way back in II Kings 2, where Elisha first picked up his master Elijah's prophetic cloak, rolled it up and struck the waters of the Jordan River with it, causing them to part so that he could pass through them. Maybe then Gehazi went on to tell about the events that follow in II Kings 2, how Elisha miraculously purified the waters of the city of Jericho, which had some kind of serious, deadly contamination. Gehazi could have provided a very long and detailed narrative about *"all the great things Elisha had done,"* eventually telling of the events of II Kings 4, the raising of the Shunammite woman's son from the dead. Resurrections are the rarest and most remarkable kinds of miracles you find in Holy Scripture, and Gehazi was in the middle of telling the king this story, and who should walk in? The Shunammite woman herself!

> *And while he was telling the king how Elisha had restored the*
> *dead to life, behold, the woman whose son he had restored to life*
> *appealed to the king for her house and her land. And Gehazi said,*
> *"My lord, O king, here is the woman, and here is her son whom*
> *Elisha restored to life."* II Kings 8:5 (ESV)

One is reminded of Humphrey Bogart's famous line as he encounters his former lover in the film Casablanca: "Of all the gin joints in all the towns in all the world, she walks into mine." What are the chances that the Shunammite would walk in at precisely this moment?

In fact, the odds of such an encounter taking place at precisely that moment are so minuscule that we have to call this a "providential conversation." The only way you could possibly have all of these factors coming together at that exact moment in time would be if the Lord were orchestrating it all and timing everything perfectly. The Shunammite woman has been living out of the country for seven years. She returned, and the very day she chose to go and seek an audience with the king—at the very hour, the very minute—the one person besides Elisha who had actually witnessed those miraculous events in her life so long before happened to be telling her story to the king. That's a "providential conversation," without a doubt!

Verse three says that she was going to the king *"to appeal for her house and her land."* In her absence, someone has taken it over. The text doesn't say who had done it, though one scholar has argued that property "left temporarily was taken over by the crown and was held in trust until reclaimed by the legal owner."[10] Possibly she went to the king because the property was in his care at the moment; or maybe she wanted him to intervene on her behalf with whoever had taken it over. In any event, the king restores the land to her, thereby providing her with a means for making a living . . . all because God had arranged for the right person to be speaking with the king at just the right moment. If Gehazi hadn't been there, the woman may have come to plead her case, but the king could easily have dismissed her as a con artist.

The concept of God's "providence" is meant to be comforting to believers. It's meant to be freeing, liberating, to know that we are entirely in God's hands, and to know that He is powerfully directing all of the events in our lives and exercising His sovereign providence over every detail. Jesus says in Matthew 10:29-31: *"Are not two sparrows sold for a penny? And not one of them will fall to the ground apart from your Father. But even the hairs of your head are all numbered. Fear not, therefore; you are of more value than many sparrows."* In other words, if God providentially arranges and directs the living and dying of such tiny and insignificant creatures, He will certainly do the same for His children, the crowning glory of His creation who are made in His image.

Scripture presents us with this doctrine of "providence" in order to calm us, to comfort us, and to give us peace and to liberate us from worry and anxiety. Scripture wants us to exult and delight in knowing that we're entirely in God's hands.

We can go one step further and say that this passage is trying to get us to see that this concept of God's providence also extends to our words and our speaking. Our conversations—the words that we speak to others and the things they say to us—they're in the hands of God too! It's not just the hairs on our heads; it's not just sparrows falling to the ground. The things that we say are also, somehow, under God's sovereign directing of all things.

The Bible places great emphasis on our speech. It emphasizes the importance of speaking truthfully and lovingly and saying words of encouragement to others. It also places an enormous emphasis on preaching—the verbal proclamation and presentation of the gospel of Jesus Christ. The things people say—speaking, preaching, our conversations—these are some of the most important avenues God uses to spread His truth, His "Word."

That's one thing our conversations do. And you see, this passage is teaching us that God is sovereign over that. He "providentially arranges" our conversations for us.

Does it ever happen to you that, after you've been in a conversation with someone, you find yourself "replaying the tape"? Especially when the conversation has something to do with the Christian faith and matters of the Gospel? Do you find yourself reviewing the details of the conversation and thinking, "Gee, I wish I'd said this . . . I wish I hadn't said that . . . I wish I'd put that a little bit differently . . . I wish I'd challenged that person when he said this or that . . . ?" Do you find yourself "critiquing your performance" in a given interchange and finding it lacking? I do it frequently; many of us do.

I'm not saying that we shouldn't be willing to admit our mistakes and learn from them, you understand. But, before we start "analyzing and critiquing" ourselves too thoroughly, we should begin by recognizing that God is entirely sovereign, even over our flawed conversations. We need to be liberated by that thought. What it means is that the Lord knows exactly whom you are going to meet. He knows precisely when those conversations will take place. He knows all the circumstances surrounding those conversations. He knows what you are going to say and how well (or how poorly) you are going to say it. If He so chose, He could prevent those conversations from ever taking place. Believe me, if a given conversation would permanently impede the progress of the kingdom of God in this world, He would intervene! He would do something if your flawed words in one single conversation will "mess up" His plans for the remainder of human history until Christ returns!

But of course, how ridiculous is it to think that some poorly chosen words on our part could throw such a wrench into the work of Christ's kingdom? Our words are important, but they're not *that* important!

Don't you find that to be a freeing thought? I do, because I am a master at "replaying the tape" on my conversations, and replaying it and replaying it far past the point of it being a constructive exercise.

Fact is, God arranges "providential conversations" for us. That's what our Scripture text is showing us. And what that means for you is that you can go into the week ahead knowing that God has already "appointed" your conversation partners. It's not merely that He knows who they are; He has specifically selected them for a purpose. He not only knows what they (and you) will say, He is providentially arranging those conversations in all their respects for some good purpose He has in mind. He's arranging them, guiding the circumstances surrounding them, preparing the perfect timing for them, so that precisely what you have to say, by His grace, is precisely what needs to be said, at the precise moment when it needs to be said. He intends to use it for His own Kingdom purposes.

That's a bit of an overwhelming thought. Psalm 139:1-6 says:

> *O LORD, you have searched me and known me! You know when I sit down and when I rise up; you discern my thoughts from afar. You search out my path and my lying down and are acquainted with all my ways. Even before a word is on my tongue, behold, O LORD, you know it altogether. You hem me in, behind and before, and lay your hand upon me. Such knowledge is too wonderful for me; it is high; I cannot attain it.*

The psalmist finds it to be an awesome thought as well: *"Even before a word is on my tongue, behold, O LORD, you know it altogether."* The Lord is in sovereign control even over the words that you say and the conversations that you engage in.

So, what should you do? How should you respond to this? Well, to start with, simply seek to be faithful in your conversations. That's one lesson: be faithful in how you speak and converse with others. Listen attentively to your conversation partners. Speak truthfully, honestly, and lovingly to them. God doesn't call you to be brilliant, eloquent, and insightful in your conversation; He just calls you to be faithful. That's all!

And if you're looking for ways to initiate some conversation with the people the Lord sends your way, a great place to start would be to find a way to start talking about "all the great things" that God has done. That's the topic of conversation in II Kings 8. The king asks Gehazi, *"Tell me all the great things that Elisha has done."* That is really asking: "Tell me all the great things God accomplished through Elisha." But don't wait for someone to make that request of you. That is not a request I often get! Instead, look for ways to bring it up yourself.

You'd have so much "conversation material" there that you could never exhaust it! If you start talking about all the "great things" that Christ has done, you will have plenty to talk about. John the apostle makes that fascinating comment at the very end of his Gospel, in John 21:25, where he says: *"Now there are also many other things that Jesus did. Were every one of them to be written, I suppose that the world itself could not contain the books that would be written."* I am confronted with the truth of John's words any time I enter my office: There isn't enough room for all the books! Things are starting to overflow and books are starting to get stacked everywhere—the room can't contain all the books that I'd like to put in there. That's the picture John is using: he's saying that the world is like an office, or a library, where all the books are about one thing—Jesus Christ and the great things He has done—and there aren't enough bookshelves to contain them all.

That's how many "great things" Jesus Christ has done. That's how much you could talk about Him; that's how much conversation material you have at your disposal.

As you enter the coming week, realize that every person you speak with was chosen by God to come your way. He has "set up your appointment calendar" so that you will have opportunities to "tell all the great things" that Jesus has done. If you do that, you will be faithful in how you handle your conversations. And, you will be surprised, and quite frequently delighted, at how the Lord will use your conversations for His glory.

PRAYER: LORD GOD, WHAT A tremendous truth it is that *"death and life are in the power of the tongue"* (Proverbs 18:1)! May that thought shape our listening and our speaking. May we, mindful of Your graciousness to us, keep our words always full of grace and seasoned with salt, so that we might know how to answer each person (Colossians 4:6). Give us the confidence to know that You have appointed all of our conversation partners for the week ahead. Use our speaking to advance Your Gospel. Help us to choose our words wisely to draw attention to You and not ourselves. We pray this in Jesus' name and for His sake, Amen.

"At least five times, therefore, with the Arian and the Albigensian, with the Humanist sceptic, after Voltaire and after Darwin, the Faith has to all appearance gone to the dogs. In each of these five cases it was the dog that died."

— G. K. Chesterton

"WHEN THE CHURCH HAS GONE TO THE DOGS"*

"For if you keep silent at this time, relief and deliverance will rise for the Jews from another place, but you and your father's house will perish. And who knows whether you have not come to the kingdom for such a time as this?" Esther 4:14 (ESV)

"And in every province and in every city, wherever the king's command and his edict reached, there was gladness and joy among the Jews, a feast and a holiday. And many from the peoples of the country declared themselves Jews, for fear of the Jews had fallen on them." Esther 8:17 (ESV)

"Now in the twelfth month, which is the month of Adar, on the thirteenth day of the same, when the king's command and edict were about to be carried out, on the very day when the enemies of the Jews hoped to gain the mastery over them, the reverse occurred: the Jews gained mastery over those who hated them. Esther 9:1 (ESV)

---

* Preached by Dr. Max Rogland at Rose Hill PCA in Columbia, SC on Reformation Sunday, 2017. Theme: We need to trust that God is in control, even when He appears absent from our lives, because He is providentially guiding all circumstances in order to deliver and bless His church.

In Douglas Adams' humorous science fiction novel, *The Hitchhiker's Guide to the Galaxy*, there is a scene involving a supercomputer called "Deep Thought." The machine's designers had created Deep Thought to be the greatest computer of all time, able to answer any question put to it. Once activated, its designers tasked it with giving them "the answer to the Ultimate Question—the answer to Life, the Universe, and Everything."

The computer tells them that it will be tricky, but assures them that it will be able to calculate the answer to the question. The designers are thrilled . . . until Deep Thought informs them that it will take seven and a half million years to run the program and come up with the answer.

After seven and a half million years of waiting, the day finally comes when Deep Thought will reveal to the human race the answer to the Ultimate Question of Life, the Universe, and Everything. Loonquawl and Phouchg, the two representatives of humanity selected to receive the answer and to relay it to the people waiting outside, sit breathlessly as Deep Thought's program reaches its final conclusion.

"Good morning," said Deep Thought at last.

"Er . . . Good morning, O Deep Thought," said Loonquawl nervously, "do you have . . . er, that is . . . ."

"An answer for you?" interrupted Deep Thought majestically. "Yes. I have."

The two men shivered with expectancy. Their waiting had not been in vain.

"There really is one?" breathed Phouchg.

"There really is one," confirmed Deep Thought.

"To Everything? To the great Question of Life, the Universe and Everything?"

"Yes."

Both of the men had been trained for this moment, their lives had been a preparation for it, they had been selected at birth as those who would witness the answer, but even so they found themselves gasping and squirming like excited children.

"And you're ready to give it to us?" urged Loonquawl.

"I am . . . Though I don't think," added Deep Thought, "that you're going to like it . . ."

"Tell us!"

"Alright," said Deep Thought. "The Answer to the Great Question . . ."

"Yes . . . !"

"Of Life, the Universe and Everything . . ." said Deep Thought.

"Yes . . . !"

"Is . . ." said Deep Thought, and paused.

"Yes . . . !"

"Is . . ."

"Yes . . . !!! . . . ?"

"Forty-two," said Deep Thought, with infinite majesty and calm.

The two men are stunned, not knowing what to make of this answer, and fall silent at first. Eventually Loonquawl explodes, "Forty-two! Is that all you've got to show for seven and a half million years' work?" The computer responds: "I checked it very thoroughly, and that quite definitely is the answer. *I think the problem, to be quite honest with you, is that you've never actually known what the question is.*"[11]

It's a humorous scene in the book but it's actually an important observation: You need to know what question is being asked before you can understand the answer that you're given.

The book of Esther is a perfect example. The book has many answers to give us, but to understand and appreciate those answers, we need to know the questions it wants to us to ask in the first place. If we don't grasp those, we will miss the real message of the book.

In the book of Esther, there are at least two key questions. The first is, "Where is God?," and the second is, "Where is the Church?"

Those are the questions the book wants us to ask, and those are the questions it answers.

The book of Esther clearly raises the question "Where is God?" Readers of the book have often commented that the word "God" is never used in Esther. From start to finish, God is never mentioned. He never acts, speaks, or is spoken to. God is, quite literally, absent from the text.

That's a strange thought if you let it sink in. If God isn't mentioned at all, and if the text doesn't mention Him saying or doing anything, then what in the world is this book doing in the Bible in the first place? It all seems so . . . secular!

But you don't have to be a philosophical skeptic or an atheist to wonder sometimes where God is. You may not deny the existence of God, but have there ever been days or circumstances when you felt as if God were absent? The psalmist certainly had such days (e.g., Psalms 10:1; 13:1; 22:1; 44:24; 89:46; cf. Lamentations 5:20). "Where is God?" is a question asked by believers and unbelievers alike. If you've ever felt like asking that question, that's okay, because this is the first question that the book of Esther wants you to ask! "Where is God?"

And what is the answer? How might a book that never mentions God's name indicate that God really is there after all?

In chapter three, Haman is able to trick the king into approving his plot to destroy the Jews. So, in chapter four, Mordecai urges Esther to intercede with King Ahasuerus, her husband. You'd think that wouldn't be a problem, but remember: Ahasuerus doesn't know that Esther is Jewish! So, Mordecai tells her, *"For if you keep silent at this time, relief and deliverance will rise for the Jews from another place, but you and your father's house will perish. And who knows whether you have not come to the kingdom for such a time as this?"* (Esther 4:14).

It's important to notice, first, that Mordecai is confident that deliverance will come from some source. Even if Esther were to keep her Jewish identity hidden in an attempt at self-preservation, Mordecai believes that deliverance would still come.

Now, how can he have that kind of confidence? Is he just an optimist at heart who sees the glass as half full? No—he's been too involved in court politics for that! No, Mordecai must have a theological basis for his hope in Esther 4:14. He can be confident that deliverance will come only if his confidence is ultimately in God and in His power and faithfulness to His people. There is no other possible way that Mordecai could say such a thing: *"For if you keep silent at this time, relief and deliverance will rise for the Jews from another place . . . ."* Mordecai has such confidence even when, on the surface of things, God seems to be completely absent. Mordecai still trusts that He is there.

The second thing to notice in Esther 4:14 is the last part of the verse. Mordecai asks Esther, *"And who knows whether you have not come to the kingdom for such a time as this?"* Timing is everything! It's vital to have the right person in the right place at the right time. If there were ever a time when it would be mighty helpful to have a pious Jewish girl married to the most powerful ruler of the ancient Near East, this would be it!

What Mordecai is saying, in effect, is: **"Your people are in need, and the Lord has, in His perfect ordering of affairs, placed you where you are today precisely so that you could do something about it."** Mordecai is making a statement about God's providence, that is: about the way that God remarkably arranges and rules the world so that situations fall into place perfectly, in ways that could never come about accidentally, by chance.

God's providence is not about His dramatic, visible, miraculous, and supernatural intervention in the normal courses of events—like when He sent plagues upon the land of Egypt, parted the waters of the Red Sea, sent down fire from heaven, raised the dead, and so on. Those are instances of God's supernatural, miraculous working. In His providential working things are much more subtle. He uses "ordinary" means, "ordinary" people, "ordinary" circumstances—but He brings them all together in ways that clearly demonstrate that His hand has been at work.

Biochemist Michael Behe and other representatives of the "Intelligent Design" movement have argued that on a molecular level living cells display an "irreducible complexity" that cannot be explained by evolution, as being the result of a process of "natural selection." Living organisms, even the smallest ones, even single living cells, require so many complex biochemical systems to be operating together simultaneously that you can never attain the picture that evolutionists try to paint, of very simple organisms developing and gradually changing and developing and evolving to more complicated organisms. Even the simplest organisms scientists observe are incredibly complicated—they are "irreducibly complex."

In a similar way, the events of Esther display an "irreducible complexity" that can only be explained as resulting from God's hand working behind the scenes. God is there, but He is working in a quiet, subtle way to put the right person in the right place at just the right time to bring about just the right result. That is the only way that the plot of Esther can be explained.

Just think about it! Could it possibly be "mere coincidence" that this Jewish woman, Esther, "just so happened" to have been the one selected by Ahasuerus out of who knows how many hundreds of women to become the Queen of Persia, at the exact time when Haman was about to begin plotting to destroy the Jewish population of Persia? Or could it possibly be coincidental that Esther—when invited in chapter five to lay her request before the king—decided to hold off for a day before making her request? And within the space of that twenty-four hours "it just so happened" in chapter six that the king had insomnia? And "it just so happened" that he selected the royal chronicles for his bedtime reading to try and fall asleep? And "it just so happened" that the particular passage he read that night recounted Mordecai's past faithfulness in saving the king from assassination earlier, back in chapter two, for which he had never been properly rewarded? And "it just so happened" that all of this managed to transpire only a moment before Haman walked into the royal court to ask the king to execute Mordecai?

Are you asking me to believe that such a combination of circumstances and events was purely accidental? Are you asking me to believe that it was just incredible luck that everything fell into place at the precise moment when help was needed? If so, you must think that I'm a "special kind of stupid" to be willing to ignore the clear message being proclaimed by such an intricately timed sequence of events. The message coming through loud and clear is that God is there, even when you can't see Him, and He is most certainly "working His plan"! And He'll bring it about at the **exact** moment it's ready, and not a minute before.

God's providence makes us wait. We have to be patient and wait while the Lord "works things out" according to His plan. And sadly, we are a pragmatic and impatient people who are more inclined to take matters into our own hands than to wait on the Lord. Abraham Lincoln once quipped, "I believe in the Providence of the most men, the largest purse, and the longest cannon," and that is probably how we think more often than we would care to admit.[12] It's much easier to walk by sight and rely on our own resources than it is to walk by faith in a God whose sovereign, providential guiding of our lives takes unexpected turns. It requires faith to wait on the Lord! And sometimes "the waiting is the hardest part," to quote the recently deceased musician Tom Petty.

"Where is God?" This is the first and greatest question posed by the book of Esther. And the second question is like unto it: "Where is the Church?"

Where is the Church in the book of Esther? The text wants you to ponder that question as well, because, honestly, the Church doesn't have much going for her. God's people are living in Susa, separated from their Promised Land and their Holy City. They have no temple, no altar, no priesthood, and their beautiful young women are being taken (perhaps forcibly) into the harem of a Gentile king. It's about as stark a contrast to the books of Ezra and Nehemiah as you will find! Ezra and Nehemiah also take place in the same post-exilic setting, roughly the same historical period. But in the book of Ezra, you have

God's people leaving their exile in foreign countries and returning to live in the Promised Land. In Ezra 3-6 they rebuild the temple and the altar and begin sacrificial worship. In the book of Nehemiah, we see God's people rebuilding Jerusalem, the Holy City. Both Ezra the priest and Nehemiah the governor cracked down on intermarriage with foreign spouses (Ezra 9-10; Nehemiah 13). Ezra and Nehemiah, in other words, sought to restore the things that served to mark out God's people as "holy" and "set apart" to the Lord. In the book of Esther, all those distinctive markers of "holiness" are gone! And so it's natural to ask the question—the question that the book wants you to ask—Where is the Church in all this? Where is her "holiness"? Where is her "set-apart-ness"?

Well, the Church is still there, not because she's doing all the things that she's supposed to be doing and living such a "holy" ("set apart") life, but simply because the Lord graciously decides to preserve her and deliver her. So, we read in Esther 9:1 that *"on the very day when the enemies of the Jews hoped to gain the mastery over them, the reverse occurred: the Jews gained mastery over those who hated them."* That's the Lord delivering His people! That's Him providentially intervening and "reversing things," "turning the tables" on the enemies of the Church. That in itself is a testimony that the Church is still to be found.

But there's more. The Church is not merely surviving all this drama; she is actually growing and thriving. In Esther, we see the Church victoriously expanding in her mission, despite the terrible circumstances. In one of the few Old Testament notices of large scale Gentile conversions, Esther 8:17 says that in the aftermath of the book's events, *"many from the peoples of the country declared themselves Jews, for fear of the Jews had fallen on them."* Don't miss that! Even in the midst of these dramatic events, *"the peoples of the country"*—i.e., Gentiles— *"declared themselves Jews."* That's referring ultimately to religious conversion to the worship of Yahweh. That's them giving up their pagan gods and goddesses and allying themselves with God's people. These people weren't born into the Covenant; they were "outsiders" making a conscious decision to enter the covenant (cf. 9:27). We're not talking about Hollywood celebrities like Madonna who think it's cool to dabble in the mysticism of Jewish Kabbalah; we're talking about people who are turning their backs on their idols and their false deities, and are embracing the one true God, Yahweh, and are becoming identified as members of God's Church.

Despite the absence of so many things that were truly important, even vital, for the life and well-being of God's people (like temple worship and sacrifice), the Church is still there and is growing. Even pagan unbelievers are turning in faith to the one true God!

G. K. Chesterton once said, "At least five times . . . the Faith has to all appearance gone to the dogs. In each of these five cases it was the dog that died."[13] The Gentiles are sometimes called "dogs" in the Bible (cf. Mark 7:27-28). In the book of Esther, God's Church is completely surrounded by and forced to mingle with Gentile "dogs." The Gentiles have the upper hand and appear to be on the verge of wiping out God's people. If ever there were a time when the Church had "gone to the dogs," this is it!

And yet it is the dog that dies. The Church isn't destroyed. It's the enemies of the Church who are defeated. The Gentiles who convert, who enter into God's covenant, receive a new identity as those who have put the old man to death and put on the new man as members of the kingdom of God.

This is one of the amazing lessons that the book of Esther teaches us: When things look as bad as they can possibly get for the Church, God in His providence surprises everyone, and He delivers His people, and He grants the Church victory!

It's a good reminder on this 500th commemoration of the Protestant Reformation. The Church was in a very bad place in the days of Martin Luther. The Church needed to be delivered and revived and restored. Her theology needed restoring. Her ministry needed restoring. Her worship needed restoring. People's lives needed to be changed. And the Lord did it, but He did it providentially: Not with big, dramatic miracles, but with an obscure monk who had spent years and years studying the Scriptures and then preaching and teaching them. There are several good biographies of Martin Luther out there, full of interesting stories. There's some drama and suspense to his life story, but it's all "non-miraculous" stuff: he didn't see visions or experience visible, dramatic, supernatural phenomena all the time. He studied, he taught, he preached; eventually he got married and had kids. He wrote letters, he wrote books. He was actually a very "down-to-earth" and "ordinary" type of guy.

You could study the other Reformers and you'd get a similar picture. The life of John Calvin, the great Reformer of Geneva, isn't all that remarkable. He was another guy who read and studied and taught and preached. He suffered with poor health and was sick a lot. In many ways, there was nothing very "special" about him. But the Lord chose to use relatively obscure and ordinary people like that to bring about something extraordinary.

The Church is always falling into hard times. She grows weak. Sometimes she loses her own way. Sometimes her enemies plot against her. But eventually, always, the Lord delivers her. The Reformation was great, but it's not like that was the last time the Lord did a work of salvation for His people. He has saved this church and many churches like her from going under. He's overthrown regimes hostile to the Gospel. He's going to save His people!

You know, the same questions get asked in every age of the Church: "Where is God?" And: "Where is the Church? Why does she seem so insignificant?" There are always circumstances that make us ask those questions. Does God appear to be absent (or at least, "vanishing") from twenty-first century American society? Sure. Has the Church lost the influence she once had on society? Absolutely. Is she a threatened, beleaguered minority in the midst of an increasingly pagan culture? Maybe so, but what of that?! It simply does not matter, because the Lord will see to it ultimately that the victory will be yours, people of God! You have been *"made alive together with Christ and raised up and seated with him in the heavenly places"* (Ephesians 2:6). You share in Christ's death, resurrection, and ascension to His throne in heaven. How will your Heavenly Father not graciously give you all things along with that? Deliverance will arise for God's people. It always does in God's providential timing. The Lord Jesus Christ is building His Church, and the gates of Hell will never prevail against her.

PRAYER: HEAVENLY FATHER, WE THANK You for the promises You have made to the Church, the Bride and Body of our Lord Jesus Christ. We thank You that, like You, we can be amused and laugh at the raging and plotting of the nations, who take their stand against Your Son Whom You have anointed as king (Psalm 2). Father, bless His reign and extend His scepter from Zion, and strengthen the Church, that we would be willing to follow Him, even in the midst of spiritual opposition (Psalm 110). Not to us, O Lord, not to us, but to Your name give the glory (Psalm 115:1)! In Jesus' name, Amen.

"Far more is involved here than simply asserting God's sovereignty. We need a way . . . for realizing the largeness of God in the midst of the competing bigness of the world."

—Eugene Peterson

"FROM WRINGING YOUR HANDS TO RAISING THEM"*

The last couple of weeks have been hard. As citizens of the state of South Carolina, we learned a week ago of the horrific shooting at Mother Emmanuel AME Church in Charleston.[14] And then, as citizens of the United States, we learned two days ago of the Supreme Court's *Obergefell* v. *Hodges* decision establishing homosexual marriage as a civil right.

Last night I went into my children's bedroom hours after they had fallen asleep. Some of you may have done that from time to time with your own children. You tiptoe in and just look at them. And you wonder, "What kind of world are they going to grow up in? How are they going to have a conscience that's not jaded? How are they going to navigate through the pressures of the world, which they will experience far more intensely than when I was their age?" Those are the kinds of questions you ponder as you see their peaceful little faces asleep on their pillows.

And as you ponder, you wonder how to pray. Over the last several days, Psalm 2 has been my prayer. Remember that the Psalms are not

---

* Preached by the Reverend Matt Miller at Greenville ARP Church on June 28, 2015, the Sunday after the Supreme Court ruling on *Obergefell v. Hodges*. Theme: Fear and anxiety about the state of society can make us cower, but the Psalms help us to be confident in God's sovereignty.

only given as God's Word to us, they also are given as words for us to speak back to God. They equip us to "answer God" in a rich, real, and reverent way. As C. S. Lewis said, "We receive (from the book of Psalms) not by using it as an encyclopedia, but by steeping ourselves in its tone and temper and so learning its overall message."[15]

Perhaps you have found yourself wondering over the last week or ten days, "How do I speak to God about these things that have happened in my state, and in my country, that have so grieved and unsettled my heart?" If so, Psalm 2 is the place to "steep ourselves," so that we can learn how to think—and how to pray—about weeks like this past one.

Let us hear God's Word:

Why do the nations rage

and the people's plot in vain?
The kings of the earth set themselves, and the rulers take counsel together,

against the LORD and against his Anointed, saying,

"Let us burst their bonds apart,

and cast away their cords from us."

He who sits in the heavens laughs;

the LORD holds them in derision.

Then he will speak to them in his wrath,

and terrify them in his fury, saying,

"As for me, I have set my king

on Zion, my holy hill."

I will tell of the decree:

The LORD said to me, "You are my Son;

today I have begotten you.

Ask of me, and I will make the nations your heritage,

and the ends of the earth your possession.

You shall break them with a rod of iron

and dash them in pieces like a potter's vessel."

Now therefore, O kings, be wise;

be warned, O rulers of the earth.

Serve the LORD with fear,

and rejoice with trembling.

Kiss the Son, lest he be angry, and you perish in the way,

for his wrath is quickly kindled.

Blessed are all who take refuge in him.

Psalm 2 (ESV)

This Psalm helps us move from anxiety about the world to worship of Him who is sovereign over the world. It takes us in the moment when we're wringing our hands and muttering in frustration, and it guides us into raising our hands in confident praise.

Maybe that's how you have found yourself recently, in that place of wringing your hands and wondering in exasperation, "What's going on in this world?" When things become more uncertain in our society, it's easy to respond in one of two ways.

On the one hand, you can decide, "You know what? I'm just going to disengage. It seems like there's nothing we can do. It seems like the forces of evil are overwhelming. So I'm just going to retreat from all of this. I'll just love my family, and I'll play golf. And hopefully before it gets really bad, I won't be around to see it. I'm just going to retreat."

But the Scriptures say that's not really a wise option. When we retreat, do you know who gets hurt? Our neighbor. As we engage in civil society and politics through voting and exercising our stewarded rights as citizens, our primary goal should be the glory of God and the good of our neighbor. When we choose to disengage from society and politics, we leave our neighbor more vulnerable to those who are choosing not to disengage.

On the other hand, we can determine, "I'm going to jump in and double down, and engage the political process in an all-consuming way. I'll invest everything I've got. I'll put every ounce of my energy into advancing certain agendas and opposing others. And people may or may not know that I'm a Christian, but they are definitely going to know my political priorities."

But you know what gets hurt when we do that? Our witness to Christ—our witness to Him as the sovereign King of kings. Our witness as believers, our core identity, is not in our political activity or party affiliation, but in our union with Christ—in all He has done for us and all that He has promised to do for us.

Or maybe you feel like you're stuck in a pinball machine, bouncing back and forth between over-engagement and retreat. An election cycle gets you ramped up and engaged, but then you come out of it disillusioned and you retreat. Then you get pulled back into the next election cycle, and you over-engage again, and you end up disillusioned and retreating again. And back and forth you go, not sure what to do.

Psalm 2 meets us in our anxiety about the world, in our uncertainty about what to do, and furnishes us with just the right language for prayer. Let's move through four parts of this Psalm.

First, Psalm 2 helps us to see the issue of God's authority. This Psalm starts with this primary question: "Why?" It takes the question that's on the tips of our tongues or in the depths of our hearts, "Why is this world such a mess?" The Psalm takes that question of ours, and it teaches us a better way to ask it: *"Why do the nations rage and the peoples plot in vain?"* The way it puts the question actually points us straight to the real issue, as well as the certain outcome.

Why is this world such a mess? Psalm 2:1 teaches us the world is such a mess because fallen, unregenerate human beings do not see

God's Word as a blessing, the way that in Psalm 1 God's Word is a path of blessing. Rather, they see it as a burden. Since they are not at peace with God through Christ, they are antagonized by His Word and authority. They would have anyone rule over them as long as it's not God. And so this *"law of the LORD"* in which the man in Psalm 1 delights, is perceived by those in Psalm 2 not as a delight, but as a burden, a constricting cord they can only think of casting off.

Do you know that the Hebrew word for *"meditate"* in Psalm 1:2 is the same word translated *"plot"* in Psalm 2:1? When you get down to the core issue of what's going on in the world, the world is divided between those who meditate on and delight in God and His authority, and those who meditate on how to get out from under God and His authority. That's the core issue!

I'm not going to go into a long exposition about the marriage issue, but in light of the *Obergefell* decision two days ago, I will share with you my conviction on the matter.

The marriage revolution in the modern world began long before the recent debate about same-sex marriage. It began in 1918 in Soviet Russia after the Bolsheviks overthrew the longstanding Russian monarch. The goal of the Bolsheviks was to rid society of God and to establish an atheistic regime. And that was the first modern nation to begin significantly changing the centuries-old definition of marriage. They wanted to demolish the institution of marriage, and they knew they could begin that demolition by removing one essential piece to marriage: "for life." So they removed it. They reduced the covenant of marriage to a mere contract or commitment that was no longer binding "for life." That was the beginning of the modern marriage revolution in our world.

This Russian atheistic view of marriage made its way into America in 1969 when California became the first state to pass no-fault divorce laws. This was a massive change to the institution of marriage in America. Here I want to emphasize that Scripture—and our Westminster Confession of Faith, following Scripture—provides grounds for divorce. Those grounds are adultery, abuse, and abandonment. But when the states, one by one, following California, began removing the requirement of grounds for divorce, they fundamentally redefined marriage in America as the Bolsheviks had redefined marriage in Soviet Russia one generation before. Within a decade, all fifty states had followed California in this radical redefinition of marriage.

It's my conviction that what we've seen in the last ten years in our nation is simply the bitter fruit of a redefinition of marriage begun more than a generation ago.

Psalm 2 reminds us that at the heart of this revolution is the basic fallen human heart that views God's authority not as something desirable, but as something that hinders the pursuit of autonomy. And so they strive to cast off God's authority, even if it leads to misery. It's true that fallen human beings would rather be autonomous and miserable, than be under God's Word and blessed.

I think of *Paradise Lost*, John Milton's famous work. When the angels rebel against the Lord in heaven, and are cast down into hell, they assemble to strategize what to do next. Taking stock of their terrible situation, Satan rallies the fallen angels with this clarion call: "Here at least we shall be free . . . Better to reign in Hell than serve in Heav'n."

That is the driving principle of fallen humanity—"better to reign in hell than serve in heaven." We easily lose sight of this and feel disoriented. Psalm 2 helps us to recover clear sight of the real issue: the sinful desire to burst the bonds of God's Word and to cast away His cords from us because we do not want to submit to God's authority.

But Psalm 2 also tells us, right there in its opening question, that the effort will not succeed: *"Why do the nations rage and the peoples plot in vain?"* That brings us to our second point.

Second, Psalm 2 helps us to see God and this world in proper scale. *"He who sits in the heavens laughs, The LORD holds them in derision"* (v. 4). Do you wonder what to make of this verse? It can sound on first hearing like God is emotionally disconnected from the pain and agony and turmoil that's happening down here on Earth and in our lives. It can sound like God doesn't really care.

But that's not at all what this verse conveys. It doesn't highlight a disconnect between God and the world's rebellion. Rather, it highlights a disproportion—it highlights that the collective attempts of the world's leaders and powers to cast off God's authority do not pose even the slightest threat to God's mighty power and purposes. As they posture and plan against the LORD, is He worried? Not at all!

Many of you remember *Gulliver's Travels*, and the memorable moment when Gulliver falls asleep in the land of the Lilliputians, the tiny little people. As he sleeps, they bring their ladders to climb his legs, arms, and torso, and work collectively to tie him down with their slender ropes. Their leader then stands on Gulliver's large chest, pokes him awake, and basically says, "Submit to us! We have you!" When Gulliver awakes, he is frightened. He feels overcome by the coordinated efforts of these tiny people.

My friends, our God is not like Gulliver! His power is infinitely greater than the sum total of all the little people who oppose Him! We know this in principle, but we fret deep down that the contest between God and all the world's powers, all the world's leaders, all the world's armies, all the world's media, might be a close one. We lose sight of how infinitely greater, how vastly disproportionate is God's strength to all the world's strength. Psalm 2 reminds us of God's infinitely greater power when it pictures Him so unthreatened, so unconcerned . . . laughing!

This is so important to remember as we enter into prayer. We need Scriptures like Psalm 2 to help us see God and the world in proper scale again. Eugene Peterson highlights this lesson, commenting on this Psalm:

> *Intimidation is as fatal to prayer as distraction. If we are intimidated, we will forfeit the entire world of culture and politics, of*

business and science to those "who set themselves . . . against the Lord."

What is at issue here is size: we require an act of imagination that enables us to see that the world of God is large—far larger than the worlds of kings and princes, prime ministers and presidents, far larger than the worlds reported by newspaper and television, far larger than the world described in big books by nuclear physicists and military historians. We need a way to imagine—to see—that the world of God's ruling word is not an afterthought to the worlds of the stock exchange, the rocket launching, and summit diplomacy, but itself contains them.

Far more is involved here than simply asserting God's sovereignty. We need a way, a convincing, usable, accessible tool for realizing the largeness of God in the midst of the competing bigness of the world. If we fail here, prayer will be stunted; we will pray huddled and cowering. Our prayers will whimper.

Psalm 2 answers our need . . . .[16]

As you hear the news, does it compress and shrink your view of God's mighty power? Then steep your soul in Psalm 2, it will open your eyes wide again to the great power of our sovereign God, who, in the words of Isaiah:

sits above the circle of the earth,

and its inhabitants are like grasshoppers; . . .

who brings princes to nothing,

and makes the rulers of the earth an emptiness.

Scarcely are they planted, scarcely sown,

scarcely has their stem taken root in the earth,

when he blows on them, and they wither . . . (Isaiah 40:18, 22-24).

The contest is not even close. God has the overwhelming power. But what is God doing?

Third, Psalm 2 reminds us of God's global purpose through His Son. *"Ask of me, and I will make the nations your heritage, and the ends of the earth your possession. You shall break them with a rod of iron and dash them in pieces like a potter's vessel"* (vv. 8-9).

To experience power in prayer, we've got to know God's ultimate purposes, so that we are aligning our prayers with His purposes. That's why the Lord's prayer is so important, as we learn to pray, "Thy kingdom come, thy will be done, on earth as it is in heaven."

What is His kingdom coming to do? What is His will here on earth? Psalm 2 trained the people of Israel to see the ultimate goal: that the Messiah will come, and the LORD will give to Him all the nations and all the peoples. God's purpose in history through its triumphs and its low points is to give a glorious gift to His Son!

They read and sang Psalm 2 waiting for the Messiah to come, waiting for Him to begin to receive that gift. We read and sing Psalm 2 in the twenty-first century. We read it as those who can see this promise of a glorious gift to the Son already "materializing." We see it not only with our very eyes, but in our very lives!

Let me ask you: how many of you have Jewish ancestry? How many of you can trace your lineage back to Abraham, Isaac, and Jacob?

It's not many.

And if that's the case, then for most of us, when Psalm 2 was written, our ancestors were not worshiping Yahweh. When Jesus was raised from the dead, most of our ancestors were not worshiping Yahweh and they certainly weren't worshiping Jesus.

Many of us have never let the real religious history of our ancestors "sink in." Many of us in this region of the country and in our denomination tend to think, "My family has been Christians for generations." Not if you go back far enough!

Let's talk about those of us with European ancestry (since we tend to think of our ancestry as "Christian"). Let's go back "far enough." If you have German ancestry, as I do, your ancestors in the first century A.D. were worshiping the planet Mercury as a god, offering to it sacrifices—not only animal sacrifices, but also human sacrifices! Some of us have ancestors who worshiped Thor. In Northern Italy and in what is today Austria, Switzerland, and France, they worshiped Belenus, the sun deity, who is often equated with the Roman god Apollo. Celtic religion also practiced human sacrifice in apparently large quantity, offering these sacrifices to the pagan god Toutatis, the protector of the tribal people. And there were the Roman and Greek gods and goddesses mingled into the worship of all those under the far reaches of the Roman Empire.

Somewhere, if you go back far enough down your family tree, there was a generation in the deep darkness of paganism (and you would probably be repulsed by how they practiced it). And somewhere along that family line, someone in your family was the first to believe that a Jew who lived in Palestine for thirty-some years in the first century was actually the Creator Himself in the flesh, the One Who made the sun and the moon and the stars that you and your people had been falsely worshiping for generations as gods. And someone way back in your line was the first to submit to the waters of baptism in the name of the Father, and of the Son, and of the Holy Spirit. Someone way back in your family line was the first to be transferred from the kingdom of darkness into the kingdom of God's beloved Son (Colossians 1:13).

God's global purpose through His Son has been at work all this time, and all of us sitting here today from our various ancestral backgrounds are living proof of that. Our ancestors would be shocked to know that we are here, worshiping Jesus of Nazareth as the Son of God! But here we are. God has been sovereign through all these centuries! And He is today, and will be forever.

Psalm 2 reminds us of God's global purpose through His Son.

Verse 9, *"You shall break them with a rod of iron and dash them in pieces like a potter's vessel . . ."* that's highlighting two things. I think the "them" that is being broken and dashed in pieces is the same as in vv. 2, 3, 4, 5 and v. 10—the kings and the rulers who have set themselves against the LORD and against His anointed, and are wanting to burst these bonds and these cords. *"Now O kings of the earth be wise, be warned O rulers of the earth"* (v. 10). It's speaking of those who persist in their rebellion against God, and in leading people into rebellion against God. Jesus will crush them when He returns!

And it will be easy for Him. At no point will the contest appear in doubt. *"Dash them in pieces like a potter's vessel,"* just thrown to the ground and shattered.

He's working out His purposes—you and I are proof of that—and He is continuing to work out His global purposes through His Son. Psalm 2 helps us see things through the perspective of God's sovereign designs.

Fourth, Psalm 2 points our worship and service to the Son, Jesus Christ.

> *Now therefore, O kings, be wise,*
>
> *Be warned, O rulers of the earth,*
>
> *Serve the Lord with fear and rejoice with trembling.*
>
> *Kiss the Son, lest he be angry and you perish in the way.*
>
> *For his wrath is quickly kindled,*
>
> *Blessed are all who take refuge in Him.*

Jesus is not an escape from politics and societal issues. He cannot be an escape from these things because He is the Messiah—He occupies the office that rules over all these things! To find refuge is to find refuge in the King of kings and the Lord of lords, concerning whom the *"kings"* and *"rulers"* of this world must be warned to *"kiss the Son."*

But finding refuge in Jesus also protects us from becoming consumed by politics, where we become known entirely by our politics, and where the intensity of our political emotion far outstrips the intensity of our worship of the King himself, to the hurt of our witness. Jesus is not an escape from the troubles of this world, but He is a real refuge amidst the troubles of this world.

When we find refuge in Him, we also find a call to serve Him. The rulers of this world are called to *"serve the Lord with fear and rejoice with trembling,"* and so are we. And how wonderful is the one we serve! Israel read their Scriptures and sang their Psalms and wondered what man would be the Christ. We read our New Testaments and see an amazing man—merciful, gentle, wise, and righteous—Who can strike fear in the hearts of the Pharisees one day, and make the woman at the well feel safe the next. We see a man, the Son of God come down from heaven, Who loved us and gave Himself for us on the Cross. And on resurrection morning, we see beyond a shadow of a doubt that He—this Jesus, this wonderful Jesus—indeed occupies the office of the Christ! It is this Jesus who rules the world! And it is this Jesus whom we are called, and privileged, to serve.

An author by the name of Kazuo Ishiguro has written a short and very stirring novel called *The Remains of the Day* (1990). If you enjoyed the TV show "Downton Abbey," this book has a similar setting and imagery. The novel is about an English butler who served a very dignified, prestigious house in England, run by Lord Darlington, during the time between World War I and World War II. It's a fictional memoir in which this butler expresses his great pride in serving such a noble man and house. Whatever Lord Darlington requested, this butler did, and he found a deep sense of identity and gratification in the service he offered this lord and his house.

The memoir takes us to three years after Lord Darlington has died, and an American has bought the house. In the midst of the transition, the butler has an opportunity to travel the English countryside for a few weeks to visit former members of the house's staff and to reflect on his own lifetime of service. But in the course of these conversations, he learns something that changes forever how he views his own life of service to Lord Darlington.

Years before Lord Darlington died, the house became, for a season, host to a number of secret meetings of English, French, and German officials. These were the years between World War I and World War II. For the butler, this was a marvelous season, serving domestic and foreign dignitaries, polishing silver for powerful men, carefully attending to their every need, and maintaining with dignity the requisite secrecy about it all.

But as the butler learned only after the fact, it was in these meetings that the Germans successfully lobbied the English for more "leash" in the post-World War I era. The results of this, if you know your history, were tragic. The reader's heart aches with the butler as he realizes that Lord Darlington, the master whom he'd so admired, was actually not so admirable, but had been an orchestrator of backchannel meetings that paved the way for Hitler. The butler was overcome with regret over whom he had served, and what tragic, epoch-making meetings he had helped "pull off."

My friends, the truth of the matter is that all of us serve someone. All of us serve something. And I want to encourage and press into your hearts today that you will never, ever, EVER! regret serving the Lord Jesus Christ! You will never regret any hard decision made for Him, you will never regret any sacrifice made for Him. And if He does call us to suffer in some way, as so many Christians in so many parts of the world and so many times in history do, you will never regret any suffering for His name.

He is the King of kings, He is the LORD's anointed, and everything is working according to His sovereign plan. Worship Him with your whole heart. Serve Him with your whole life! Psalm 2 sends us forward in faithful service to our Lord Jesus Christ.

Psalm 2 helps us to see the issue of God's authority, it helps us to see God and the world's power in proper scale, it reminds us of God's global purpose through His Son, and it raises us from our knees to go out and face the world, giving our worship and service to our glorious Lord and Master, God's Son, Jesus Christ.

PRAYER: HEAVENLY FATHER, HELP US to rejoice in Your sovereignty and power, and to discern Your plan for the nations, and to rejoice that we who trust in Christ are now part of Your great gift to Your Son. And I pray that when fear and anxiety begin to compress our view of You, that Your Word—and especially the Psalms—would open wide our eyes to Your majesty, and fill our hearts with Your strength, that we would be those who don't cower, who aren't intimidated, but are able to rejoice and serve the Son all the days of our lives. We make this prayer in Jesus' name, Amen.

Section Two

SERMONS FROM THE NEW TESTAMENT

"Evil is not merely the absence of good, nor is it a stage in man's upward development; it is a terrible enemy of human well-being and will never be outgrown or abandoned until God has mightily intervened to purge evil from the earth."

—George Eldon Ladd

"HOPE IN THE FACE OF THE HERODS OF THE WORLD"*

After they (the Magi) had left, an angel of the Lord appeared in a dream to Joseph and said: "Herod will be looking for the child in order to kill him. So get up, take the child and his mother and escape to Egypt, and stay there until I tell you to leave." Joseph got up, took the child and his mother, and left during the night for Egypt where he stayed until Herod died. This was done to make come true what the Lord had said through the prophet, "I called my Son out of Egypt." When Herod realized that the visitors from the East had tricked him, he was furious. He gave orders to kill all the boys in Bethlehem and its neighborhood who were two years old and younger—this was done in accordance with what he had learned from the visitors about the time when the star appeared. In this way what the prophet Jeremiah had said came true: "A sound is heard in Ramah, the sound of bitter weeping. Rachel is crying for her children; she refuses to be comforted, for they are dead." After Herod died, an angel of the Lord appeared in a dream to Joseph in Egypt and said, "Get up, take the child and his mother,

---

* Preached by Dr. Loyd Melton at Cedar Springs ARP Church in Bradley, SC on December 29, 2013. Theme: We face the reality of evil in the world, but Jesus by His life, death, and resurrection has overcome the power of evil.

and go back to the land of Israel, because those who tried to kill the child are dead." So Joseph got up, took the child and his mother, and went back to Israel. But when Joseph heard that Archelaus had succeeded his father Herod as king of Judea, he was afraid to go there. He was given more instructions in a dream, so he went to the province of Galilee and made his home in a town named Nazareth. And so what the prophets had said came true: "He will be called a Nazarene." Matthew 2:13-23 (TEV)

For most, Christmas is such a season of joy. The laughter and the glow in children's eyes as they look forward to it is infectious even to those of us who are quite cynical because of the commercialization of the season. The songs about Jesus' birth and the carols that we sing have a way of piercing through the bitterest and hardest of hearts.

Ironically, it's also sometimes a time of great sorrow and despair. On December 25, 2011 in Stamford, Connecticut, a fire broke out in a home shortly before 5 a.m. In minutes, the whole house was engulfed in flames killing a mother, father, and three children. The mayor of Stamford said: "There probably has not been a worse Christmas Day in the city of Stamford." A few days before Christmas in 1929, Charlie Lawson, a tobacco farmer from Stokes County, North Carolina, took his wife and seven children, ranging from seventeen years to four months, into town to buy new clothes and have a family portrait made. Given the fact that they were a poor, struggling family, this was most unusual. On Christmas Day, 1929, he shot and killed his wife and six of his seven children, and then killed himself.

Tragedies like these unfortunately happen far too frequently, but their happening at Christmas makes them seem even worse. It is utterly amazing how realistic the Bible account of the birth of Jesus really is. We become so moved by the miraculous things such as the shepherds being visited by the heavenly angels, the dreams through which God speaks to Joseph, and the Magi seeing a special star, that we fail to see the sheer reality of evil. Nowhere is evil seen any clearer than in Herod's brutal order to have the little Jewish boys in and around Bethlehem murdered.

The Herodian dynasty ruled over Palestine from around 40 B.C. until about A.D. 100. Probably the worst of them was Herod the Great who is mentioned in our passage. After his death, Palestine was divided and the different parts were ruled by his sons: Archelaus, Philip, and Herod Antipas. Herod the Great came to power around 37 B.C. when he was twenty-five years old. In many ways, especially during his early years, he was an effective ruler. He built theaters, amphitheaters, and hippodromes. He constructed military fortresses to protect the people of Judah. Perhaps his most fabulous building achievement was the Temple in Jerusalem. His primary motive for rebuilding the Temple was probably to appease the Jews who were resistant to his rule because he was not a Jew. On at least two occasions, he reduced taxes just to appease the Jews.

Yet, he was heartlessly cruel. After he was appointed king, in an effort to consolidate his power, he confiscated the property of forty-five of his wealthiest and most powerful enemies and had them executed. He had two of his own sons executed. His last years were spent in fear and paranoia over his throne. In all, he had ten wives and each one wanted her son to succeed him. He changed his will six times.

The scene described in our Scripture passage is corroborated in no other source. Yet, many scholars who have spent their lives studying Herod have said that such an insane, brutal act is the very kind of thing that Herod did in his latter days. The contrasts in this scene are quite as nonsensical as a family that perishes in a fire on Christmas morning or a man so angry or desperate or both that he murders most of his family and himself on Christmas Day.

Amid all the joy, cheer, and goodwill of the Christmas season, we must never forget that the world into which Jesus came and in which we live is one in which many Herods dwell. They are alive and well and just as vicious and deadly as Herod the Great. The life of our nation and indeed of the whole world was radically changed on

September 11, 2001. Today, there are few sectors in our lives that are devoid of security cameras. The process that one must go through now to board an airplane has forced many to decide not to travel anymore. We've come to expect on the nightly news—as almost routine—to hear accounts of mass shootings, heartless cruelty, and unspeakable loss. Herod still lives in our world, and he still wreaks havoc with our lives.

If we aren't careful, the realness of the world's Herods will make us become fearful, timid, anxious, cynical, and bitter and can cause us to withdraw from the world and wait for the new world to come. At the very time when Herod orders this murderous act against the baby Jesus, there existed not too far away a group of very strict Jews who had withdrawn from public life, probably in the second century B.C., and had gone to one of the most remote, lifeless, and miserable spots on Earth—the Dead Sea. Most scholars believe they were the Essenes. They were probably a group of very strict Jews who wanted to take Palestine back from the corrupt Seleucids who were trying to force Jews to compromise with pagan Greek culture. This conflict erupted into the Maccabean Revolt which occurred from 167 to 164 B.C. and ended with these conservative Jews winning and getting back control of Judah, Jerusalem, and the Temple. Their victory is the basis of the celebration of Hanukkah today.

Even after the victory, the control of their land and temple which they had regained, and a national and spiritual revival, the Essenes still saw elements of uncleanness, unfaithfulness, and compromise. Their world was still Herod's world—still too spiritually filthy for them to live in it. So, they withdrew and sought to form a pure community near the Dead Sea where they would not be tainted by the moral rot of the world around them. They would wait for God to bring in the new world after the final battle of history. The great gift which the Essenes gave us is the Dead Sea Scrolls. Among the scrolls are a group of works which describe the Essenes' daily life as well as their thoughts about what was happening in their world. In reading these works, we see clearly that in their worldview, the Herods of the world were becoming bigger and more threatening, and their hope became less and less attached to this world and more and more focused on the world to come.

Is that not where many of us Christians find ourselves today? As the violence and bloodshed that we read about becomes more and more common, and at the same time increasingly bizarre and unexplainable, do we not conclude that our only hope is for Jesus to return and bring an end to the world's madness? I think it is significant that some of the recent more popular TV series focus on people who have chosen to live their lives in remote sections of Alaska where they are far removed from the Herods of the world. Think of the popularity of "Doomsday Preppers" where people have chosen to live in the fortresses they have constructed in anticipation of the dissolution and destruction of society that is sure to come. Think of how many tons of freeze-dried rations with a guaranteed shelf life of twenty-five years must have been sold in anticipation of what many thought would happen when the year 2000 rolled around!

Herod's order is neither the first nor the last time that evil attempts to thwart God's purposes. We see it in Genesis 3 in the clever words of the serpent who tempts Adam and Eve by twisting what God has said. We see it in the Pharaoh of Egypt who probably laughs in Moses' face when this fugitive from Egypt dares to relay to him God's demand that he let His people go. We see it in people like Jezebel who is determined that the worship of Baal will replace the worship of Yahweh in Israel and vows to silence Elijah's voice who has dared to oppose her.

The battle that Joseph faces is not new. Notice how the deck is stacked against him. Here's Joseph, who was an ordinary Jewish man in remote first century Palestine, just trying to protect his family against King Herod, a vicious, ruthless madman who has a whole army at his disposal. It's like a top-five college football team that schedules a small Division II team for one of its "creampuff" games on its schedule. It's not a game—it's a scrimmage!

Joseph is told by God through a dream to retreat to Egypt. While Egypt was the place of slavery and oppression for his forefathers, it had become a refuge for Jews who needed to flee from Palestine. For centuries, there had been a thriving, welcoming community of Jews in Egypt. Tradition has it that Jeremiah went there sometime after the fall of Jerusalem in 586 B.C. and lived out the rest of his life.

Sometimes, retreat on the battlefield is the wiser course of action. We need the wisdom of God to know when it's time not to engage in battle. A pastor was once confronted after the morning worship service by an angry parishioner who accused him of talking about him before the whole congregation in the sermon. Very wisely, the pastor convinced the man to go home and think about the situation. He promised to visit the parishioner the next day and they would talk about his concerns. The next day came. The pastor went by and the man apologized profusely saying that he was dealing with some personal problems for which he was ashamed, and he mistakenly believed that everyone in the church was talking about him behind his back. He now realized that it was his own guilt and shame that drove him to the outburst and that the pastor had done nothing wrong. This encounter provided the pastor the opportunity to listen to and offer wise counsel to this troubled brother. I remember well a fellow pastor from many years ago who found himself moving quickly from one church to another because he seems never to have learned that solving every conflict with the "bull in the china shop" approach is not always the best course of action!

Retreat is not always a bad thing. Sometimes, it is the wiser course of action. During those months or years that Joseph waited in Egypt, we can only imagine what he thought. He was in a foreign land and far away from family, friends, and all that was familiar. Yet, he waited for God to act.

We spend so much of our Christian pilgrimage waiting for God to act. Waiting is not "down time" or wasted time at all. We must never forget that our perspective on life is always partial and skewed, but God sees it all from beginning to end. When it appears that our lives are shut down by evil and that there is no foothold in the swamp, God is acting to accomplish His purposes for His creation and for us. At a time when Judah had fallen to Babylon, Jerusalem had been devastated, and the people of Judah had been taken into exile with no hope of ever returning, God spoke to them through a letter from His prophet Jeremiah saying to them: *"I alone know the plans I have for you, plans to bring you prosperity and not disaster, plans to bring about the future you hope for"* (Jeremiah 29:11, TEV).

Like all tyrants and dictators, Herod died. Jewish tradition maintains that when the Jews heard of his death, they took to the streets and danced. Josephus tells us that after his death, Palestine broke out with armed Messianic revolts everywhere so that Herod's troops had to move in to put them down. Yet, things didn't change a whole lot. Herod's kingdom was divided among his sons who essentially continued the oppressive measures of their father. Verse twenty-two tells us that when Joseph heard that Archelaus had replaced his father, he was still afraid to go home. Again, God speaks to Joseph in a dream and instructs him to go to Galilee which he does and settles in a small village called Nazareth. Joseph comes back into Herod's world.

The child would group up in Nazareth. At around thirty years of age, He would begin His public ministry in Galilee teaching, healing, casting out demons, and preaching. In His preaching, He would announce the dawn of the Kingdom of God and call for repentance in preparation for it (Matthew 4:17). He would preach to huge crowds made up mainly of common, ordinary people in Galilee who were aware every day of the realness and the terror of evil. While most in those crowds put their hope in a time someday in the future when God would put an end to evil and bring in a new age, Jesus preached about a Kingdom that was not just future but was present, here and now. His healings and His casting out demons were signs of that Kingdom's presence here and now.

There will always be Herods in the world who work to take away anything that is decent, good, and wholesome. We confront our own individual Herods in our lives as we deal with the complex, twisted, and painful human dilemmas that are part of our everyday living. As a pastor, I have thought often about some of the life situations of the people whom I serve and have wondered to myself if I could ever find enough strength and courage to live under those circumstances. When confronted with the Herods of the world, we can always retreat and try to remain out of Herod's reach. This almost always fails. Or, we can remember that through our faith in Jesus Christ, we are already living in another Kingdom—where through His death and resurrection, He has already conquered evil, death, and hell. We, living in Herod's world, can live new lives out of that victory. In a world that is filled with tragedy, sorrow, and suffering, we can live as people of hope because the ultimate upending of all the Herods of the world has already been accomplished on the first Easter.

PRAYER: O GOD OF OUR Lord Jesus Christ, how we thank You that in our dark world we can live as people of hope. Renew that hope and the power and presence of Your Spirit in our lives that those around us may see and be drawn to the hope within us that is Your gift to us. In Jesus' name we pray, Amen.

"Mercy=empathy plus action."

—Unknown

"MERCY MULTIPLIED"*

"Blessed are the merciful; for they shall obtain mercy." Matthew 5:7 (KJV)

The nineteenth century was *the* century for Christian missions. The Yale historian Kenneth Scott Latourette wrote a five-volume history focusing exclusively on Christian missions in the nineteenth century. One of those Christians who felt God's call on his life to pursue the life of a missionary was John Patton. Specifically, Patton felt called to the island chain of the New Hebrides between Hawaii and Australia. Two earlier missionaries to the New Hebrides in the 1840s were sacrificial lambs. They were killed within minutes of leaving their boat, and the cannibals subsequently dined on the fresh meat.

Despite the objections of his friends, John Patton landed with his pregnant wife in the New Hebrides in November of 1858. Four months later Mrs. Patton gave birth to a healthy baby boy, but three weeks later she contracted a fatal fever and died. The infant son caught his mother's fever and died ten days later. John Patton also caught the fever, but miraculously survived to dig two shallow graves for his wife and baby.

Patton spent the next four years pouring his heart and soul into ministry on the islands only to be driven out by the people. Patton,

---

* Preached by Dr. Dale Johnson at Calhoun Falls Presbyterian Church on February 19, 2017. Theme: The Lord's mercy, grace, and providence are relentlessly given to us every day as gifts from a bountiful God.

however, did not give up on his call to missions. He raised support for four years, re-married, and convinced his new bride to follow him to the same islands where he had buried his first wife and son.

John Patton began his mission career again, armed with a new strategy. He and his bride started an orphanage and over time, trained thousands of children in the catechism. God blessed these efforts beyond their wildest hopes. By the year 2000, 85 percent of the residents of the Wala archipelago were Christians! Mercy bore fruit.

Against common sense and all odds, what drove missionary John Patton? He nearly drowned in despair and desperation, but returned to a cannibal people not with rage and hatred in his heart, but in fact with divine attributes of love, mercy, and grace. Someone has defined mercy as "empathy plus action." You see a need and are moved by that need to respond in action. Mercy comes more naturally to some than others. I wish I had more mercy! I wish I was more merciful. I see brokenness and hurting people and I say, "Why doesn't somebody do something about this?" Merely recognizing the need is not mercy. Mercy is stepping out and getting your hands dirty in someone else's messy life.

Mercy is a central biblical theme. In Matthew 5:7, Jesus could not be more precise: *"Blessed are the merciful; for they shall obtain mercy."*

In God's great mercy, He does not give us what we deserve; rather, He gives what we *do not* deserve. He gives us mercy. I have heard people say, "I just want a fair shake from God. I just want what's coming to me." NO, NO, NO, a thousand times NO! If God dealt fairly, justly, equitably, we would all suffer torment and punishment from God. We absolutely do not want a "fair shake" from God; instead, we want mercy and loving-kindness. Justice would send us to Hell. Mercy gives us what we do not deserve.

There are times in our lives when we are at wit's end. We don't know what to say except to cry out to God, "Be merciful unto me, O God, a sinner!" Have mercy, O God, have mercy! This is how we find

David in Psalm 25. He is not just in a pickle, *he* is a mess and his *life* is in a mess. Psalm 25, verses 1-7 reveal this.

> *To you, O LORD, I lift up my soul. O my God, in you I trust; let me not be put to shame; let not my enemies exult over me. Indeed, none who wait for you shall be put to shame; they shall be ashamed who are wantonly treacherous. Make me to know your ways, O LORD; teach me your paths. Lead me in your truth and teach me, for you are the God of my salvation; for you I wait all the day long. Remember your mercy, O LORD, and your steadfast love, for they have been from of old. Remember not the sins of my youth or my transgressions; according to your steadfast love remember me, for the sake of your goodness, O LORD!*

Specifically note verses 6-7 where David appeals to God's tender mercies. *This* is what we want, not justice or fairness.

I am not a big movie-goer, but as I prepared this sermon, a movie was "playing" in my mind. The movie is titled *Tender Mercies*. It stars Robert Duvall who won his only Oscar for Best Actor for his leading role in 1983. Duvall plays a character named Mac Sledge, a recovering alcoholic and country music singer, who seeks to turn his life around through his relationship with a young widow and her son in rural Texas.

There are several important themes in the movie—the importance of love, family, and redemption which we see in Mac Sledge's conversion to Christianity. There are admittedly many theological issues which cloud the word conversion here, but this is probably the best we could hope for from Hollywood.

Shortly after his marriage to the young widow, Rosa Lee, Mac begins attending the local Baptist church where Mac and Sonny, his young step-son, were baptized. After baptism, riding home in Mac's old pickup, Sonny asked Mac whether he feels any different? Mac replied, not yet! This probably indicates Mac's belief that God's mercy and grace will lead to meaningful changes in his life. There is in fact hope for the future, because God is merciful.

Horton Foote, the screenwriter of *Tender Mercies,* chose the title of the movie from Psalm 25:6. He chose the title with the Rosa Lee character in mind. Her first husband had been killed in Vietnam. In the movie, Rosa Lee does not want grandness, fame, or notoriety. She seeks only moments of gentleness and tender mercy. Mac Sledge came into her life and filled that role. In one scene Rosa Lee tells Mac, "I say my prayers for you and when I thank the Lord for his tender mercies, you are at the head of the list."

One critic reflecting on that line paralleled Rosa Lee's words with those of the Apostle Paul in Romans 12:1. Paul writes, *"I appeal to you therefore, brothers, by the mercies of God, to present your bodies as a living sacrifice . . . to God."* In other words, live your life in service to others. Invest in people. People are more important than things.

In the Sermon on the Mount, Jesus said, *"Blessed are the **merciful** for they shall obtain **mercy**."* Mercy is empathy and compassion plus action. We should exhibit this attribute because it is another way of summing up the law.

God the Father gave His only Son and took pity on a fallen rebellious people who deserved wrath, but received mercy through Christ who took our sin upon Himself. *"For our sake he made him to be sin who knew no sin, so that in him we might become the righteousness of God"* (II Corinthians 5:21). **That is mercy!** Mercy cost the Father the life of His only Son.

There is a story behind the sermon title—"Mercy Multiplied." For my family, the title and the story are personal. Three years ago the Johnson household was not just in chaos—it was in crisis. It was a living hell. Our daughter, Taylor, was diagnosed and was battling a deep, deep depression. She was losing the battle, and we were losing our daughter. At one point she was on eight medications. Getting out of bed was an enormous struggle. Merely putting on shoes was a nearly impossible task. We simply gave up the demand that Taylor wear shoes—it was not worth the battle. On those rare days when Taylor got out of bed, she left the house without shoes through the entire winter of rain, sleet, or snow.

I didn't really understand depression when she was diagnosed, and I don't really understand it now—but I do know all of my well-intended efforts, pep talks, pats on the back, encouragement and rebuke to "snap out of it" was all for naught. My constant prayer seemed to go no higher than the ceiling. She had a hard heart and would listen to no one, certainly not her parents. Counsel was given, prayers and tears of family and friends were offered. Promises were made and broken. Lessons were not learned.

When Taylor went out at night, we didn't know when she would come home or if she would come home. There was theft, the emptying of my checking account, lying, and a clumsy suicide attempt. Taylor was spiraling out of control. There was despair and no hope. Counseling and medications proved worthless. Perhaps she learned that alcohol and prescription drugs do not mix. The most difficult part for me, personally, was Taylor's self-harm. She was a cutter. She began cutting her forearm leaving dozens of long scars. I learned that cutters do this because they are completely numb. They feel nothing. Cutting is a deliberate attempt to *feel something, anything!* The pain of cutting gave her the rare sensation of at least *feeling something!*

Now with that as background, let's turn the corner of despair. In the providence of God, we found a place of hope. This place took in young women who were facing the entire variety of life's challenges. They dealt mostly with eating disorders, drug addiction, alcoholism, abuse, and depression. The place we found was called "Mercy." Mercy Ministries (now Mercy Multiplied) is headquartered in Nashville with centers in Mississippi, Missouri, Canada, and elsewhere.

At Mercy, Taylor found herself and her identity, because she found Christ. She found the Lord and Mercy saved her life. For nearly a year Taylor lived in a setting without cell phones, television, or computers. She learned to write letters. She learned to make her bed. She learned to wear shoes! She had one primary task—to heal through confession, prayer, repentance, worship, immersing herself in Scripture, and following the advice of godly counselors. She learned to love God!

On weekends, Taylor was allowed to make a few phone calls. One Saturday, she called me and said to me, "Dad, I have a favorite verse of Scripture." This was a remarkable admission on her part but I was skeptical to say the least. I fully expected her to quote, "Jesus wept," or John 3:16 or something else. She said, yes, it is from the Old Testament. I was still skeptical, but intrigued. She continued, yes, the verse is from the prophet Ezekiel. Ezekiel 36:26-27, *"A new heart also will I give you, and a new spirit will I put within you: and I will take away the heart of stone and I will give you a heart of flesh. And I will put my spirit within you, and I will cause you to walk in my statutes, and you shall keep my judgments and do them."*

As I listened to her quote these verses from memory, I could hardly steer the car. I was witnessing a miraculous answer to prayer. What Taylor did not know, was that I had been praying and claiming Ezekiel 36:26-27 on Taylor's behalf for over two years. Of all the verses the Lord put on her heart, it was the passage I prayed over and over again for her. The Lord did indeed remove her heart of stone and give her a new heart. He put a new spirit within her. Through His divine mercy, she was grafted into the family of God! Thank God for His tender mercies. His mercies are new each morning.

PRAYER: O GOD OF ALL mercy, we give thanks that You being rich in mercy, because of the great love with which You loved us, even when we were dead in our trespasses, You made us alive together with Christ. Help us to be merciful, that we may obtain mercy, in Jesus' name, Amen.

"God is always doing 10,000 things in your life, and you may be aware of three of them."

— John Piper

"DISAPPOINTED IN THE LORD"*

And Jesus went away from there and withdrew to the district of Tyre and Sidon. And behold, a Canaanite woman from that region came out and was crying, "Have mercy on me, O Lord, Son of David; my daughter is severely oppressed by a demon." But he did not answer her a word. And his disciples came and begged him, saying, "Send her away, for she is crying out after us." He answered, "I was sent only to the lost sheep of the house of Israel." But she came and knelt before him, saying, "Lord, help me." And he answered, "It is not right to take the children's bread and throw it to the dogs." She said, "Yes, Lord, yet even the dogs eat the crumbs that fall from their masters' table." Then Jesus answered her, "O woman, great is your faith! Be it done for you as you desire." And her daughter was healed instantly. Matthew 15:21-28 (ESV)

Disappointment. Henry David Thoreau, in a discussion of life's many disappointments, wrote "The mass of men lead lives of quiet desperation." I think it fair to say we all live lives with some level of disappointment, and many of our disappointments are, in the great scheme of things, small. Years ago, I was doing my weekend duty with the Army Reserve. As was my practice, I left at lunch to drive into

---

* Preached by Dr. R. J. Gore Jr. at Church of the Good Shepherd in N. Augusta, SC on August 20, 2017. Theme: God is good, and cares for us more than we can imagine—even in those times and places when He appears unresponsive to our pleas for help.

Greenville to the Little Pigs Barbecue on Pleasantburg Drive. As I drew near, I noticed there was no smoke coming from the chimney. They smoked pork shoulders with hickory wood, and I was concerned that there was no visible evidence of smoking! As I pulled into the parking lot, I saw a sign posted, thanking everyone for their patronage, and noting that the restaurant was closed after thirty-five years. I had been a customer off and on for twenty-five of those years—and I was very disappointed!

Other disappointments are more profound—and sometimes our disappointment goes beyond the immediate circumstances to the Lord who has appointed those circumstances. One of the greatest disappointments in my lifetime was the terrorist attacks on 9/11. I was not only disappointed in our government, and the massive intelligence failures, I was disappointed in the Lord— that He would allow such a thing. I realize that such thinking is shallow and simplistic, but it is a human tendency, isn't it, to attribute blame to the Lord and find fault with the way He is running the show.

Indeed, the Bible is filled with people who were disappointed in the Lord. Think of Mary and Martha in John 11. They sent a message to Jesus, letting him know that his good friend Lazarus was deathly ill. Jesus responded by doing nothing, just staying put for a couple of days. By the time He decided to visit Bethany, Lazarus was dead and his cold body was in the tomb. Jesus then told His disciples that He was glad, for their sakes, that He had not gone to Bethany! In Luke 9, the disciples were on their way to Jerusalem when they ran into opposition from some Samaritan villagers. James and John responded to this by asking Jesus if He wanted them to call down fire from heaven to destroy the wicked Samaritans. To their disappointment, Jesus rebuked them for their haste and lack of grace.

I think it is fair to say that Job was disappointed in the Lord. The Scripture tells us God commended Job for his faithfulness and obedience. In fact, Job was the great example of faithfulness that God held up before Satan. But that faithfulness didn't have much of a payoff, did it? You remember how that worked, right? A messenger ran up to Job and all his friends sitting at the gate of the city and told him that all his children, servants, flocks and herds were gone; all that was dear to him—destroyed. What a payoff! Don't you think Job was disappointed in the Lord? Indeed, he was, and he spends most of the book complaining to the Lord.

Perhaps more to the point, I am confident there are people in this congregation who have been disappointed in the Lord, for one reason or another. Perhaps life has not turned out the way you expected; your path has been difficult, and you wonder, "where are the promises of His blessing?" Disappointments come in many forms, not merely as injustices committed, or proper justice delayed. In this vale of tears, disappointments can come from a doctor's visit, a strained family relationship, a financial setback, a text message from a wayward child, or a breaking news alert on the TV. Or from not receiving an email, text message, or phone call—just silence.

In his book on suffering, D.A. Carson writes these words: "One of the major causes of devastating grief and confusion among Christians is that our expectations are false. We do not give the subject of evil and suffering the thought it deserves until we ourselves are confronted with tragedy. If by that point our beliefs—not well thought out but deeply ingrained—are supremely in Jesus, then the pain from the personal tragedy may be multiplied many times over as we begin to question the very foundation of our faith."[17] It is because we believe in the absolute goodness of God, and the omnipotent power of God, that we struggle with the pain of life's disappointments.

In that light, let me ask this: Is your faith "robust enough that, when faced with excruciating adversity," though you "lash out with hard questions," you stay the course and do not "turn away from God."[18] Now, we are supposed to trust the Lord. But, trusting the Lord does not mean you don't get angry. It doesn't mean you don't have questions. Jesus, the God-Man, dying on the cross for the sins of the world, uttered the Cry of Dereliction: "Why?" "Why have you forsaken me?"

Yet, in the end, He trusted His Father and committed to Him His Spirit. D.A. Carson writes we must always trust in the Lord even "when he can at best be only dimly discerned behind events and circumstances that the Bible itself is quick to label evil."[19]

Now, returning to our text, do you realize that just about everyone in the narrative was disappointed in the Lord? Earlier in the chapter, Jesus had engaged in open conflict with the Pharisees over their hypocrisy and faithlessness. They were disappointed that Jesus did not keep their religious traditions. They asked him pointedly, "Why do your disciples break the tradition of the elders? They don't wash their hands before they eat." The Pharisees reasoned that God was pleased with externalities. Be of the right racial stock; wash your hands; keep the traditions that have been passed down. These are the things that really matter.

Jesus responded by correcting their bad theology. He called them hypocrites and blind leaders of the blind. *"It is not what goes into a man's mouth that defiles a person,"* Jesus said, *"but what comes out of the mouth"* (Matthew 15:11). Eating with dirt on your hands does not make you unclean in God's sight. Instead, *"what comes out of the mouth proceeds from the heart, and this defiles a person. For out of the heart come evil thoughts, murder, adultery, sexual immorality, theft, false testimony, slander"* (Matthew 15:18-19). These things, manifested outwardly, spring from a heart made unclean by sin.

Jesus distanced Himself from the Pharisees by His teaching. And, after this exchange, He also distanced Himself physically from the Jews. He left Galilee to travel about thirty miles northward in the direction of Tyre and Sidon, a Gentile stronghold. These cities were situated in the general vicinity of modern Beirut. The inhabitants of those lands were called "Phoenicians," a word that comes from the Greek word for Canaanite. Canaanites were the inhabitants of the Promised Land, the wicked people who were supposed to be destroyed by Joshua's invading forces. They were notorious for their worship of many gods and their depraved religious practices. When Jesus drew near to this region, a

Canaanite woman, a descendant of these wicked people, came to Him begging for mercy. She asked Jesus to deliver her daughter from demon possession. Literally, "she kept on crying to Him," asking Him for help.

Think about that. Delivering someone from demon possession appears to be all in a day's work for Jesus. Matthew had already recorded that Jesus had healed two demon-possessed men, one in chapter eight, and the other in chapter twelve. Besides, according to Matthew 14:35-36, Jesus had been quite busy, healing people from the surrounding countryside, people afflicted with all sorts of problems. So, all things being equal, she wasn't asking for the moon and the stars. She wasn't even asking for a personal favor—she begged Jesus on behalf of her daughter whom she loved. We read that Jesus did not even acknowledge her request. The New Living Translation reads *"he gave her no reply—not even a word."*

Well, this Canaanite woman was disappointed. She had addressed Jesus as Lord, quite likely a term of devotion, since she also called him by the Messianic title, *"Son of David."* These expressions suggest that she was familiar with the Old Testament. She may have heard about His teaching, perhaps even knew some of the people He had healed. She knew this much: she had a need and she knew that Jesus could help. And, considering what she did know about Jesus, she expected anything but cold, icy silence. So, she came to Him, as Mark's account tells us, on behalf of her *"little daughter"* (Mark 7:25) as *"soon as she heard about him."* Surely this one who had done so much for others could do something for her! But, when Jesus finally spoke, He brushed her off, callously stating that He was sent only to help the lost sheep of Israel.

Now, wouldn't you have done something to help her if you had been there? If you had the ability? Can you identify at all with this Canaanite woman? Have you ever spent a sleepless night in a hospital waiting room? Watching the clock tick, second by second, so agonizingly slowly. Or been at your wit's end, with needs you cannot meet, problems you cannot solve, troubles that only the mighty hand of God can resolve? Have you ever been rudely awakened at two in the morning with news that breaks your heart? Have you ever prayed about something that was ripping you open, and felt that your prayers were bouncing off the ceiling tiles and going no higher? That was the Canaanite woman's experience, and her heart ached with disappointment.

The disciples also heard this woman's cries for help. They noted Jesus' silence and were themselves disappointed in the Lord. But not because Jesus failed to help this poor woman. Apparently, they gave no thought to her problem at all. No, they just wanted her to be quiet. She was a nuisance. They wanted Jesus to send her away at once and to put an end to the noise. In a sense, you can understand this, can't you? Everywhere Jesus went, the crowds pressed in and the cries rang out for Jesus to stop and heal someone from some malady. Day after day without respite; no doubt the disciples grew weary of the constant badgering. Well, something similar happened in our text, but this Canaanite woman would not stop. When Jesus did not answer her cry for help, she did not have the good manners to cease and desist. The disciples just wanted Jesus to put an end to this embarrassing and irritating scene. They *"kept on urging him"* to send her away, and were disappointed when He did not act to end this scene.

With neither Jesus nor the disciples showing any concern at all, her disappointment should have been enough to send her packing. But this poor woman was shameless, and proceeded to act out one of the most pathetic scenes in the Bible. Throwing herself at Jesus' feet, she cried out, *"Lord, help me."* At this point she had identified herself completely with her daughter's need. In her mind, her needs and those of her daughter had become inseparable. Apparently still unmoved by her tears and desperation, Jesus replied to her that it would be inappropriate to take the children's food and give it to the dogs. The Jews typically viewed themselves as God's children and considered the unclean Gentiles to be nothing more than dogs. Jesus used the very language that was common among the Jews and by that language appeared to endorse their arrogance and exclusivism. But His intent was otherwise.

It is at this point that the woman responded in a remarkable manner. Her spirit was vexed, and her heart was broken. But she would not turn aside. In humility, she acknowledged herself to be unworthy. But even as she accepted Jesus' apparent dismissal of her as a dirty Gentile, she reminded Him that even the little housedogs ate crumbs that fell from their master's table. And, we find something amazing in our text. In response to her final plea, Jesus now addresses her disappointment. He said, *"Woman, great is your faith! Let it be to you as you wish. And her daughter was healed that very hour!"*

What a contrast between the Canaanite woman and the Pharisees! The Pharisees were the children of the covenant. They had the oracles of God, lived in the land of Promise, and the Anointed One Himself stood in their midst. But with all their privileges, the Lord was disappointed in them. They despised the very Bread of Life set before them. Unlike His seeming indifference to the Canaanite woman, Jesus had frequently offered Himself to His own people. But now, in our text, Jesus speaks not words of comfort, but condemnation. He accused the Pharisees of drawing near with their lips while their hearts were far from Him.

The Canaanite woman, however, was the exact opposite. She was a foreigner to the covenant of God. She lived in the land of the covenant breakers under sentence of death. Yet she drew near with her heart and hungered for the Living Bread. And as her heart drew near the Savior, so with her lips she sought mercy—and Jesus gave it to her. Not at first, mind you, for He withheld outwardly what He intended to give her inwardly. Jesus disappointed the Canaanite woman in order to bless her in the end. At first Jesus ignored her with His lips in order that at last He might draw her heart close to His heart.

This has often been the experience of God's people. Think of how long Abraham and Sarah waited for the promised son, Isaac. Think of the many times the Psalmist cried out, "O Lord, how long?" And think of the other examples we find in the New Testament. Why did Jesus delay to heal the blind men in Matthew 9? Why did He take so long before responding to Jairus whose daughter lay dying on her bed? Why did He delay those two days in Bethany, letting Lazarus slip from sickness to death, John 11:6?

In C.S. Lewis' *The Lion, the Witch, and the Wardrobe*, four children, Peter, Edmund, Susan, and Lucy, are transported to the magical land of Narnia. Narnia is a strange place with talking animals and an evil witch who has cursed everything so that it is always winter and never Christmas. And, in Narnia, there is Aslan, the Great King, the Christ Figure who brings redemption to the land of Narnia. Aslan, of course, is a great Lion, "the King of the wood, and the Son of the Great Emperor Beyond the Sea." When the four children hear about Aslan, they are quite frightened and one has the bad form to ask, "Is he [i.e., Aslan]— quite safe?" Not quite getting a clear answer, one of the children again seeks for clarity: "Then he isn't safe?" said Lucy. "Safe?" said Mr. Beaver; "Don't you hear what Mrs. Beaver tells you? Who said anything about safe? Course he isn't safe. But he's good. He's the king, I tell you."

Now, let me confess. The Lord has disappointed me, just as He disappointed Mary and Martha, Lazarus, and Job. Just as He has disappointed every one of us on so many occasions. But consider this. Although He disappointed Mary and Martha, at the end He restored Lazarus to life, strengthened the faith of the disciples and caused many of the Jews to believe on Him. He did heal the blind men. And He took Jairus' daughter by the hand, saying "Little girl, rise up." The Lord did not deliver Stephen from stoning, but He was there to welcome Stephen when he stepped from this life into the next. God does not act on our timing, but He is never late for a divine appointment. He does not always act as we want, but He always acts as we would want Him to act **if we only knew what He knows and could see things as He sees them.**

How has God disappointed you? Has He ignored your desperate pleas for help? Has He responded to your loud cries and groanings with a deafening silence? Has He let the tears flow while you knelt helplessly at His feet? Do not waste those tears. When God knocks the props out and removes the arm of flesh, do not let your trials be in vain. James says, *"The testing of your faith develops perseverance. Perseverance must finish its work so that you may be mature and complete, not lacking anything"* (James 1:2, 3). None of your trials is accidental, and no disappointment is without divine purpose. They are all part of God's plan to make you die to yourself and to become more like Jesus.

As we have seen in our text, when the Lord turns a deaf ear to us, He does so to draw us closer to Himself, so that we may hear Him clearly when He does speak. When He ignores our cries for help, it is only to teach us what we need to ask of Him. When the Lord disappoints you, it is not out of malice or indifference, but out of love. We do not understand His ways, and there are many things that puzzle us. But this much we know: when He disappoints us, it is not to hurt us, but to teach us that He alone is our joy, our contentment, and our all-sufficiency. As C. S. Lewis wrote, He isn't safe. But He is good. He's the King, I tell you.

PRAYER: ALMIGHTY GOD AND HEAVENLY Father, clouds and thick darkness are all around You; righteousness and justice are the foundation of Your throne. Indeed, Your ways are not our ways, but we trust You, confident that the judge of all the earth will do right. Teach us to bear the disappointments of life, confident that through it all, You have plans for us, plans for peace and not evil, to give us a future and a hope. This we pray through Christ our Lord, Amen.

"We should ask God to increase our hope when it is small, awaken it when it is dormant, confirm it when it is wavering, strengthen it when it is weak, and raise it up when it is overthrown."

—John Calvin

"PRAY . . . AND DON'T GIVE UP"*

And he told them a parable to the effect that they ought always to pray and not lose heart. He said, "In a certain city there was a judge who neither feared God nor respected man. And there was a widow in that city who kept coming to him and saying, 'Give me justice against my adversary.' For a while he refused, but afterward he said to himself, 'Though I neither fear God nor respect man, yet because this widow keeps bothering me, I will give her justice, so that she will not beat me down by her continual coming.'" And the Lord said, "Hear what the unrighteous judge says. And will not God give justice to his elect, who cry to him day and night?, Will he delay long over them? I tell you, he will give justice to them speedily. Nevertheless, when the Son of Man comes, will he find faith on earth?" Luke 18:1-8 (ESV)

The NIV reads this way: *"Jesus told his disciples a parable to show them that they should always pray and not give up."* Other translations say, *"and not to faint,"* or *"not to lose heart."* I think the NIV removes any possible ambiguity: *"Pray, and not give up."* The story is a simple one and at some level resonates with everyone here today. We are all good Americans.

---

* Preached by Dr. R. J. Gore Jr. at Boyce Memorial ARP Church in King's Mountain, NC on September 30, 2012. Theme: God is always at work in our lives, using circumstances to teach us to pray and trust His good plans for our lives.

We embrace the underdog, the righteous cause, the rags-to-riches, up-by-the-bootstraps efforts of individuals who just will not give up. Our heroes are Bill Gates and Steve Jobs—and the little engine that could. There is some of that in this story. But there is much more, and if we only see the celebration of dogged determination, we have missed much that is important in this passage.

There are two characters in the parable. The first character is a judge, a man whose very title defines not only his vocation, but also the qualities he is supposed to bring to his office. We speak of those who have a proper "judicial temperament" and lengthy discussions take place in the Senate over whether nominees for high courts have such a disposition. What do we expect from a judge? Well, a judge is one who discerns what is right, dispenses justice, avenges injustice, and rights wrongs. But this judge cares nothing about God. In the Old Testament, the fear of the Lord is described as the beginning of knowledge and the beginning of wisdom. Yet this judge does not fear God, nor does he reverence Him—and so for those hearing the story, this judge would be reckoned not a wise man, but a fool who has neither knowledge nor wisdom. He is completely lacking proper judicial temperament. That might make him a good fit on the Ninth Circuit Court of Appeals, the most overturned appeals court in the United States, but he is far short of what the Bible demands from a leader of God's people.

Furthermore, this judge has another characteristic of a fool. He is arrogant and unteachable. He cares nothing for what others think. The phrase, *"cares nothing,"* has a couple of possible meanings. It can mean that the judge has no regard or respect for other people. This would be an awful situation indeed, for a judge who has no respect for others is not one you could count on if you have suffered an injustice. Or, it could mean that he is not ashamed of his actions before other people. This man, who is supposed to uphold right and suppress wrong, cares nothing for the rights or opinions of others. He has no shame before those whose well-being he is supposed to protect; this judge is not embarrassed by his own unjust behavior.

The second character is a widow, probably a woman of few means and little political or social standing. While we are given no details of her situation, apparently someone has taken advantage of her lowly status. She does not ask for special privilege or extraordinary consideration. She simply asks for justice, for what is right. But she asks this of a judge who has no regard for justice and cares nothing at all about public appearances or perceptions. He can afford to ignore her pleas for help. He already has a bad reputation; he has accepted that fact, and her squalling will not make him any worse in the public eye.

But something unusual happens in the interaction of these characters. The widow just will not go away. Like the slow drip of Chinese water torture, she chips away at the judge's resistance. She takes every opportunity to cry out for justice. This judge couldn't go to the grocery store or the gas station without the widow showing up, crying out, and making a scene. Like the professional demonstrators we have seen all too much, there was no escape. Now the judge was not concerned with what people thought. But no one likes to put up with continual harassment. Like the mother in a toy store who finally buys something for her three-year old—just to make him be quiet—the judge decided to give justice to this woman before she wore him out. Not because she deserved justice. Not because it was the right thing to do. Not because he cared for those who were helpless. He ruled for the plaintiff simply to get her off his back.

Then Jesus said, *"Listen to what the unjust judge says. And will not God bring about justice for his chosen ones who cry out to him day and night? Will he keep putting them off? I tell you, he will see that they get justice, and quickly."* Think of the contrasts: God is the righteous judge, whose holiness demands that He always act in accordance with His righteousness, not an unjust judge who cares nothing about right and wrong. Jesus says His chosen ones, His elect, are those **beloved** by the Father from the foundation of the world; not a poor widow, alone and unloved by all in the world. And Jesus says, God will answer their prayer—and quickly! This argument uses the form of a standard Jewish way of reasoning; if this, then so much more that. If an unjust judge will begrudgingly hear the plea of a nobody who will not go away, how much more will your righteous Heavenly Father hear and answer the cries of His children whom He dearly loves, indeed, whom He has loved from eternity.

But there is one basic requirement of our text, demonstrated by the poor widow's persistence—that is, that you will pray and not give up. The widow did not receive her answer right away. Yet she did receive justice eventually because she would not quit. And Jesus uses this story to remind us that we ought always to pray. In fact, the word here is very strong. Jesus says, *"it is necessary for men always to pray."* While there are many prayers in the Bible, and numerous references to prayer, no text is more important than the Lord's Prayer. And, consistent with our Gospel text for today, the repetitive nature of prayer is emphasized in the Lord's Prayer, as Jesus instructs his disciples to pray for their *"daily bread."* So when Jesus tells the disciples, *"pray, and don't give up,"* He is consistent with His teaching elsewhere on prayer. And He is not encouraging vain repetition, as though mouthing words repeatedly is important, but rather encouraging persistence in prayer.

But someone might ask, "Why pray?" God *"works out everything in conformity with the purpose of his will,"* as Paul says in Ephesians 1:11. If that is true, and it is, why should we pray? Isn't God going to do what He plans to do anyway, regardless of my prayers or yours? Well, that is a good question, but it really is beside the point. The same Scripture that says God will accomplish all that He purposes, is the same Scripture that says, *"it is necessary"* for us always to *"pray and not give up."* So, whether I am able fully to satisfy in my own mind the relationship between God's sovereignty and prayer, I have been told to pray by the sovereign Lord Himself! And that ought to be enough.

But having said that, there is yet more that we can say about prayer. Just as God determines all the ends that He wishes to accomplish, even so He determines the means needed to accomplish those ends. In my former duties as an Army officer, I spent a lot of time thinking about strategic affairs at the national and international level. One of the things I learned is this: the first thing a good strategist does is determine the desired end-state, or ultimate goal. With that in mind, it is possible to marshal your resources, establish a sequence of events, and orchestrate the ways and means needed to reach the desired end. Now, God could have chosen to accomplish all things on His own. He did not, but instead has seen fit to make our prayers one of the means whereby He accomplishes His will. And in the process, those who pray receive enormous blessings!

Now, let's ask another question: what is it we do when we pray? Are we trying to get stuff from God? A superficial look at this passage might give that impression. When I was a teenager, I used to hear Janis Joplin sing, "O Lord, won't you buy me a Mercedes Benz." And that is often our approach to prayer. We want something from God, and so we pray and ask Him for it. And if we are really serious, we fast and pray about it. And in certain theological circles, we get others to agree with us so we can claim God's blessing. Now! But, is that what prayer is all about? Is prayer really an automatic guarantee that God, like Burger King, will let you have it your way?

I don't think so. For example, James warns us against self-centered prayers. He says, *"You do not have, because you do not ask God. When you ask, you do not receive, because you ask with wrong motives, that you may spend what you get on your pleasures"* (James 4:2,3). Furthermore, the Lord's Prayer gives us some idea of how prayer ought to be focused. Look at the petitions: *"Hallowed be thy name. Thy kingdom come. Thy will be done, on earth as it is in heaven."* These petitions focus on the Lord, praising Him and seeking the success of the kingdom of God and the will of God on earth—and in our lives. Only afterwards are we instructed to pray for ourselves. And we ask for **daily bread.** Not to win the lottery, or to have a freezer full of food. We ask for what we need this day—not for the whole week, month, or year. And we ask for those things that are necessary—not all the "wants" on our Christmas gift list or Amazon wish list. And, as we ask for daily sustenance, we also ask for daily cleansing—*"forgive us our debts"*—as we pray that we might have a forgiving spirit towards others. Our final petition is for deliverance from the power of evil, or as some translate it, *"the evil one."*

Now, as I look at the Lord's Prayer, it seems that there is very little in this prayer about my needs, and nothing at all about my wants. I don't think there is anything necessarily wrong with telling God what you want, but you must remember that you are on thin ice if telling God what you want is the heart and soul of your prayer life. Prayer is not so much telling God what you want Him to do. It is rather opening yourself up to Him so that you become aware of what **He** wants to do in your life. Remember how Jesus prayed in the Garden? *"Lord, let this cup pass from me!"* That is what He wanted. But He knew it was more important that He receive what His Father wanted for Him. And so He added, *"Nevertheless your will be done."* That is why we pray that God's kingdom will come in our midst, that His will be done, here and now, the very same way it is done in heaven.

But, there is something else in this text that gives us an idea of how we ought to pray. What motivated the widow to cry out to the unjust judge? Why, her circumstances! She found herself in a situation where she had been deprived of justice. She needed a redress of grievances. Her circumstances forced her to seek relief from one who had both the authority and the power to grant that relief. And so it is often with us, that circumstances drive us to focus our prayers. Let's be honest; it is awfully hard to pray with authenticity, *"give us this day, our daily bread,"* in our safe, ordered world. After all, you can pray for your daily bread, or run down to the grocery store with a couple of bucks and buy a loaf whenever you want.

But things are different in the hard times, aren't they? Perhaps not as bad as the first century world, where one bad crop could plunge the whole country into famine. But we live in a world where hurricanes rampage, and tornadoes drop from the sky. We do not face the dangers that our soldiers face in Afghanistan where IEDs randomly explode, and Taliban terrorists torment and kill unarmed civilians. But every day there are a multitude of unseen threats that might harm you. And I will confess to you that in times of physical distress or personal difficulty, I am motivated to pray more earnestly than when I am sitting snug and secure in days of comfort. Jesus said we ought always to pray and not quit. And sometimes our God-ordained circumstances make it easy to obey this command.

Perhaps you are thinking, I don't like to think about uncertainty. I don't want to think about the threats that are out there, such as economic woes, high rates of unemployment, disease, or long-term disabilities. Perhaps you just want to live your life, make ends meet, and take care of your family! Many of you have seen "The Lord of the Rings" movies, or read the books. Perhaps you feel a bit like Frodo when he found out that the Ring he received from his uncle, Bilbo, was the Ring of Power that was being sought by the Dark Lord himself. "I wish it need not have happened in my time," said Frodo. "So do I," said Gandalf, "and so do all who live to see such times. But that is not for them to decide. All we have to decide is what to do with the time that is given us."

So what **do** we do with the time that is given us and the uncertainties we all face? Among other things we *"pray and do not give up."* We ask for God's blessings in the midst of life's uncertainties. We ask that His rod and staff comfort us and guide us. Now, I know what some of you are thinking. But what if He doesn't answer my prayers? Every day I ask Him to watch over me and to protect me—and to protect my family and friends. I ask for guidance and direction in my life. I pray that God will keep our soldiers safe, but every day I read about soldiers who are killed. And there are car wrecks on the evening news, random acts of violence in our major cities, tornadoes in Alabama, drug cartels warring in Mexico, and floods and droughts throughout the United States. All of this bad news can have an effect on us. From 1988 to 2008 there was a 400 percent increase in the number of Americans on anti-depressants and today over 11 percent of all Americans over age twelve are on antidepressants. I suspect there are many who are thinking, "I just don't know what to do. I am overwhelmed and not even sure God hears my prayers."

Do you ever wonder if God *hears* your prayers? Well, of course He does, if by that you mean, does God know what you are asking for and understand your request. But, there is a bigger question: if God "hears" your prayers, does that mean He will answer your prayer requests? After all, doesn't Scripture say: *"Ask and it will be given to you; seek and you will find; knock and the door will be opened unto you?"* Indeed, Scripture says exactly these words, but these words are predicated on the condition that what you are requesting is compatible with the will of God. God always does for us what is best, and always gives us what we need—even when it appears that He is not present, has not heard us, or is taking His own sweet time.

Let me make this crystal clear. God always hears your prayers and always answers. Sometimes He says, "Yes!" and answers immediately, giving you just what you requested. Sometimes He says, "Yes!" but this is not the best time. You need to wait a bit until the timing is perfect. So be patient and at just the right moment your prayer will be answered. Sometimes He says, "No," this would not be best for you. I have something better in mind. Keep praying and as you do I will work in your heart to get your prayers in line with My will. Now, this can be the hard part. Getting our prayers in line with His will. You see, it is all right to pray, "Lord, give me good health and long life to serve You." But it is better to pray, "Lord, let Your will be done in my life, and if that includes good health and long life, I will be grateful." It is good to pray, "Lord, watch over my loved ones." But it is better to pray, "Lord, watch over my loved ones—but Your will be done." And yes, I know this is hard to do.

Think for a moment of the great heroes of faith mentioned in Hebrews chapter eleven. These were men and women of faith—and they knew how to pray! But there is something remarkable about these heroes. Some triumphed because of their faith, while others suffered in spite of their faith. Listen to the words of Scripture.

> *And what more shall I say? I do not have time to tell about Gideon, Barak, Samson, Jephthah, David, Samuel, and the prophets, who through faith conquered kingdoms, administered justice, and gained what was promised; who shut the mouths of lions, quenched the fury of the flames, and escaped the edge of the sword; whose weakness was turned to strength; and who became powerful in battle and routed foreign armies. Women received back their dead, raised to life again. Others were tortured and refused to be released, so that they might gain a better resurrection. Some faced jeers and flogging, while others were chained and put in prison. They were stoned; they were sawed in two; they were put to death by the sword. They went about in sheepskins and goatskins, destitute, persecuted and mistreated- the world was not worthy of them. They wandered in deserts and mountains, and in caves and holes in the ground. They were all commended for their faith . . . .* (Hebrews 11:32-39)

Some of these heroes overcame by escaping bodily harm and death; other heroes triumphed by undergoing bodily harm and, for some, untimely death. Don't you believe that God heard the prayers of ALL of these great heroes of the faith?

Edith Schaeffer, wife of Francis Schaeffer, reflected on this passage in her book, *Affliction*. She suggested there are two trophy cases in heaven. In Trophy Case A are all the saints who have been delivered from trials and tribulations. Daniel from the lion's den. The three young men from Nebuchadnezzar's fiery furnace. And many other examples that displayed God's power to deliver. They are all there as trophies, testaments to God's grace and His ability to answer prayer and deliver them from dangerous circumstances.

In another display, Trophy Case B, are identical situations—except for one thing. In this second display case are all the saints who were thrown to the lions and slaughtered, who were tortured, who were burned at the stake or otherwise put to death. They are all there as trophies as well, but as testaments to God's grace to accompany His people through their deadly circumstances—and God's ability to answer prayer according to His will. God could have delivered them. He did not. But, He was with them nonetheless in their suffering. Jesus asked to be delivered from the cross. God could have delivered his Son. He did not.

And so Jesus, *"who for the joy that was set before him endured the cross, despising the shame, and is seated at the right hand of the throne of God."* He *"offered up prayers and supplications, with loud cries and tears, to him who was able to save him from death, and he was heard because of his reverence. Although he was a son, he learned obedience through what he suffered. And being made perfect, he became the source of eternal salvation to all who obey him"* (Hebrews 5:7-9). He was obedient unto death, even the death of the cross, and now God has exalted Him on high and given Him a name that is above every name. The blessed cross is the ultimate trophy of God's ability to take that which is most dreadful in the moment and, by His mercy and grace, turn it into triumph, and joy, and blessing.

Dear brothers and sisters, no one here knows what God's will for tomorrow will be. And so we pray. For that matter, no one knows whether you will make it home from church today, or whether you will have a job next week. And so we pray. No one knows if our college and career-age young people will go on to lead wonderful, fruitful lives, or struggle to find employment and happiness; whether we will enjoy good health in the golden years, or suffer the ravages of the aging process. We do not know whether in the moment our cup will overflow, or be poured out empty; whether God will shut the mouths of the lions, or let us become the blue plate special. And so we pray with hope, and don't give up.

But as you pray, pray also with confidence—and not fear. And, never lose sight of the fact that Jesus now intercedes for His people. As my mentor, Dr. Clair Davis writes, "What I'm trying now to do in my prayers, somewhat forced but still genuine, is to remember to say something like this: Father, I rejoice that You understand what I'm talking about, what I'm groaning about—because Jesus is telling You. Father, I rejoice that You hear me because You hear Him, your faithful and loving Son. Father God, You have kindly given Him to me as my loving Mediator, so this prayer isn't wasted, not at all." And so we pray with confidence, and don't give up. In the beautiful words of William Cowper, the hymn-writer:

> *You fearful saints, fresh courage take*
>
> *The threatening clouds you so much dread*
>
> *Are big with mercy, and shall break*
>
> *In countless blessings on your head*

So, let us all ask boldly for what we desire—and pray earnestly for God's blessings upon our family, friends and even for ourselves. Let us pray that God will be with us, and help us now and in the hour of our need. Let all of our circumstances, whether good or bad, lead us to pray. And let our prayers lead us to accept the will of God for our lives. I cannot tell you what the will of God is for my life, much less for yours. But that He loves us, is beyond doubt. That He is wise is beyond dispute. That He is kind beyond all measure, is demonstrated in countless blessings every day. Pointing to the story of this widow who kept "knock, knock, knocking on heaven's door," Jesus said in words as relevant to us today as to His original audience then, *"Men ought always to pray and not give up."*

PRAYER: ALMIGHTY GOD AND HEAVENLY Father. Teach us to pray. Use our circumstances to make us men and women of prayer. Use our brokenness, fears, illnesses, and disappointments to teach us to turn to You in prayer. Use our triumphs, victories, blessings, and joys to teach us to give thanks to You in prayers. In all our being and doing, help us to pray and not give up. Through Jesus Christ, our Lord, our great Mediator and Intercessor, we pray, Amen.

"Faith and patience, like two stars, shine most bright in the night of desertion."

—Thomas Watson

"A DOXOLOGY IN THE DARKNESS: TRUSTING JESUS' PRAYER WHEN FACING LIFE'S PAIN"*

John chapter seventeen unveils, in a unique and most personal way, the "deep, deep love of Jesus." But in John 17:20-26, we come to see that love for you *personally*. Today I believe that those hearing my voice may be given the faith to trust—that He is there in your marriages, that He is there in your parenting, that He is there in your days in school . . . and for some of you simply that *He is just there*. Open your Bibles and read with me from the Old Testament, in Psalm 112:4, then Isaiah 42:16, before turning to our text in John 17:20-26.

> *Light dawns in the darkness for the upright; he is gracious, merciful, and righteous.* Psalm 112:14 (ESV)

> *And I will lead the blind in a way that they do not know, in paths that they have not known I will guide them. I will turn the darkness before them into light, the rough places into level ground. These are the things I do, and I do not forsake them.* Isaiah 42:16 (ESV)

---

* Preached by Dr. Mike Milton at Trinity Chapel (ARPC) in Charlotte, NC on August 20, 2017. Theme: Is it possible to sing amid the shattered dreams of life? John 17, the high priestly prayer of the Lord Jesus, reveals a promise and brings His presence giving sustaining power—even overcoming power—to those enduring the darkness of affliction.

"I do not ask for these only, but also for those who will believe in me through their word, that they may all be one, just as you, Father, are in me, and I in you, that they also may be in us, so that the world may believe that you have sent me. The glory that you have given me I have given to them, that they may be one even as we are one, I in them and you in me, that they may become perfectly one, so that the world may know that you sent me and loved them even as you loved me. Father, I desire that they also, whom you have given me, may be with me where I am, to see my glory that you have given me because you loved me before the foundation of the world. O righteous Father, even though the world does not know you, I know you, and these know that you have sent me. I made known to them your name, and I will continue to make it known, that the love with which you have loved me may be in them, and I in them." John 17:20-27 (ESV)

Let us pray.

Let the words of my mouth, and the meditation of my heart, be acceptable in thy sight, O LORD, my strength, and my redeemer. Psalm 19:14 (KJV)

Is clarity necessary for faith? Is perfect understanding a sign of one's stronger belief in God? The brilliant ethicist, Reverend Professor John Kavanaugh, S.J., went to work for three months in the "house of the dying" in Calcutta seeking for answers on how to spend the rest of his life. Mother Theresa was still alive then, carrying the crippled, pouring oil onto the wounds that would never heal, and giving dignity to a people who are called outcasts. John Kavanaugh, on his first day there, went to Mother Theresa. "And what can I do for you?" she asked. Kavanaugh requested prayer from the Albanian nun. The saintly Mother Theresa replied, "What do you want me to pray for?" The scholar replied, "Pray that I have *clarity*." Mother Theresa countered quickly and with resolution, "No, I will not pray for *that*." With confused surprise to this abrupt answer by this tiny "holy woman," John

Kavanaugh asserted, "Why not?" And Mother Theresa told him, "Clarity is the *last thing* you are clinging to and must let go of." Kavanaugh complained that she seemed to have clarity and understanding in abundance. And he wanted it, too! She laughed and said, "I have never had clarity; what I have always had is trust. So, I will pray that you trust God."[20]

So, too, I do not ask if you have full understanding. I ask, "Do you have trust?" Do you trust in Christ and in His Word and His promises to you? I bring this matter before you because it is now time to move beyond trying to understand the unfathomable depths of meaning of John 17 to the most important place. Do you trust this Savior who prays for you? Understanding must yield to trust. And trust is another thing altogether.

Today I want to show you that Jesus' prayer is that you will, indeed, trust in Him. I do not use the word "believe," though that is the word we use in John 17:20. He prays for those who will believe. But I use the word trust. In the Greek New Testament, there is one word used whether our English puts it "believe" or "trust." We have, I think, abused the word "believe." We live in a culture where to believe in Jesus has possibly become something different than the New Testament usage of the word. There, to believe is to be aware of your powerlessness and helplessness in the face of your sinful condition and the fallen condition of the world. And it is, as the late theologian Richard Niebuhr puts it, not only to acknowledge the historical person of Jesus, but also His "authority" over all your life.[21] It is to transfer your trust from anything or anyone else to Jesus Christ alone.

But my concern this morning is how you come to do that. And taking into consideration that there are probably thousands of reasons that could keep you from receiving His authority over all your life, I want you to see John 17 and verses 20-26. For in these verses, something amazing is at work and it is this: Jesus has already taken the first step towards you. And I make my main proposition as clear as I am able:

You can trust in Jesus for Jesus has prayed for you to trust in Him. He did this in three remarkable ways in this passage.

1. Jesus prayed for you before you were born. This is what is meant in this passage when we read that Jesus says, I pray not only for these but for those who will believe through their testimony. In other words, Jesus was praying for people who had not been born yet! And so, too, did this God say to young Jeremiah: *"Before I formed you in the womb I knew you, before you were born I set you apart; I appointed you as a prophet to the nations"* (Jeremiah 1:5). This likewise accords with Paul in his letter to Ephesians: *"For he chose us in him before the creation of the world to be holy and blameless in his sight. In love"* (Ephesians 1:4). And, *"he predestined us to be adopted as his sons through Jesus Christ, in accordance with his pleasure and will"* (Ephesians 1:5).

Our Savior, too, is praying for His little ones not yet born. Now that sounds funny perhaps, except when you know that all the time, I do that and you do that. We have several couples who are expecting right now. I am praying for two families expecting their child through the wonder of adoption. I am also praying for couples who are expecting a child that the wife is carrying, but let us consider, for a moment, the couples waiting on God's choice for them through adoption. They are praying for the child that God has chosen for them before the foundation of the earth. They are praying for safety in birth, for divine guidance in the whole matter of the paperwork through the state, and of course for the day when that baby will be placed in their arms. At that moment, it will not matter what has gone before. All the waiting, even the pain they have experienced as a couple, will evaporate in the presence of the heat of love and the first cry of their new child for food. We are praying for someone not even born.

This is what Jesus was doing. And after this prayer, and after looking over a city that would reject Him, and riding into a city on the back of a donkey, hearing cries of "Hosanna" which would become cries of "Crucify Him!" Jesus counted it all worth it. He counted it all worth it because He loved His little ones. He loves you. And you can trust our Lord, no matter your pain, no matter the pain you see in the world, because He first loved you. He loved you before you were born. Now in this passage, we see that Jesus not only prayed for you before you were born, but another thing:

2. Jesus prayed for you before He died for you. This prayer happens prior to the Crucifixion. And to know this is important. It is important that you know that you were chosen in Christ before the foundation of the world and that Your Savior called out your name to His Father in His life. And therefore, His death is for you. He prayed for you, trusted in one day possessing you and therefore He died for you. He did not die and then beg you to believe. He chose you, He prayed for you, and then He died for you. Your salvation is not dependent upon your choice of God but His choice of you.

    "You did not choose me, but I chose you and appointed you that you should go and bear fruit and that your fruit should abide, so that whatever you ask the Father in my name, he may give it to you" (John 15:16).

    ". . . no one can come to me unless the Father has enabled him" (John 6:65).

Now these are amazing words with mysterious meaning. But rather than theorizing about the mystery let's see the practical power of this truth. That Jesus prayed for you before He ever died for you means the end of despair for you who are struggling to find faith; for you who are longing to trust. For you who have been abandoned by family, hurt by friends, brutalized by the rat race, or deeply moved by a world of suffering and pain, this Jesus is already on your side. He does not require that you get those questions answered and then come to you. He comes to you amid the pain and loves you. You come then when you know that love. That is what I want to preach to you most today: the love of Jesus that would love you and pray for you and value you above His own prerogatives for divinity; above His own sinless life. He was willing to be handed over to evil men, to be ridiculed, to be abandoned by God on the stinking and smoldering landfill called Calvary *so that He might save those He loves.*

To know this and experience this prayer of Jesus for you, will not only set you free who are longing to trust Jesus, but will bring happiness to sad hearts of disciples who have forgotten the wonder of His love for you. Brennan Manning in his book, *Ruthless Trust,* tells of a time when he was speaking in 1999 at Stanford University in Palo Alto, California. He had addressed faculty and students about the grace of God in Christ, focusing on the love of Jesus. The next day a distinguished faculty member came to him. She talked to him and told him this:

"At one point in my life I had a faith so strong that it shaped the very fiber of each day. I was conscious of God's presence even in stressful situations. The fire of Christ burned inside me." Slowly, . . . and almost imperceptibly . . . she told how that fire had gone out. She told how academia and life and stuff just crowded out trusting in Jesus. After a moment she continued, "After you spoke on the love of God last night, I cried for an hour. My life is so empty . . . I'm like Mary Magdalene in the garden crying, 'Where has my Beloved gone? I miss God so much that sometimes I feel frantic. I long for the relationship I used to have.'"[22]

Do you feel like Mary Magdalene, "Where has my Beloved gone?" The truth is He is alive. And He died and rose again not to beg you to accept Him. While you were still a sinner, Christ died for you. And before He died for you, He even prayed for you. You can then trust Him or trust Him again. Your Beloved is here. Now all of this in John 17 comes down to this: Jesus not only prayed for you before you were born, and before He died for you, but something more:

3. Jesus prayed for you, though today some of you do not want to pray to Him. You see you have yet to come to realize what Jesus Christ already plans for you. What I must make clear to

you from this passage is that your unbelief or your lack of trust does not intimidate God, nor will the Father deny Jesus' prayer for you to trust in Him because now you are in sin, or you are confused, or you have troubles of the soul. No, my beloved, God is like Michelangelo who saw David in rocks when others only saw boulders. This whole magnificent chapter is about the step that God has taken to you before you ever took a step at all. He chose you, He loved you, He prayed for you, He died for you, and He believed in you. The Swiss theologian Hans Urs von Balthazar stated: "We need only to know who and what we really are to break into spontaneous praise and thanksgiving."[23] This is not man-centered narcissism; it is God-induced wonder at a love like no other. David has this wonder of how God loved him. David, in his sin and his shame and his failures, could yet exclaim:

I praise you, for I am fearfully and wonderfully made . . . (Psalm 139:14a).

Or as Eugene Peterson paraphrases it:

I thank you, High God—you're breathtaking! Body and soul, I am marvelously made! I worship in adoration—what a creation! (Psalm 139:14).

Now let us be clear. The answer to the prayer of Jesus for your holiness is not up to your intellectual prowess or good breeding. No. He trusted in His oath and covenant and blood. He trusted in the design of His Heavenly Father who chose you in love. He knew His mission on Earth, and on the cross, would be successful because the Spirit would regenerate your dead spiritual heart and cause you to pant after Him. Again, this trust is way beyond anything you could imagine. It is rooted in the divine love of God for Himself and thus for His creation. That is the force of this great chapter. But when you know that He trusts in you, He loves you—it does something. It transforms you. Jesus' trust that you will be His transcends your circumstances which seek to resist or oppose that love.

The Devil in the Book of Job is saying to God, "Sure, old Job is a fine specimen of a godly man now, but just let him lose everything! Then the truth will come out! He is only as good as the blessings. When they go, he will go."[24] But God trusted in His own plan for Job and could thus trust that nothing would separate Job from God. Not even heartache. And amidst all the Hell that Satan could send, at the end of all the shallow theology of his so-called friends who told him that "you are in this fix because of your sin," Job shouted out the trust that was born out of God's Word to Him:

> *Oh, that my words were written! Oh, that they were inscribed in a book! Oh, that with an iron pen and lead they were engraved in the rock forever! For I know that my Redeemer lives, and at the last he will stand upon the earth. And after my skin has been thus destroyed, yet in my flesh I shall see God, whom I shall see for myself, and my eyes shall behold, and not another. My heart faints within me* (Job 19:23-27).

I often illustrate what I see in Scripture from my own life because I know that best! I can never forget my Aunt Eva, who raised me, telling me, "Son, just because you are a Protestant, don't you ever think bad of Roman Catholics." Now I will tell you why she said that. She told me that when my Daddy was sinking low in alcoholism, and the darkness of that sin and disease had taken his career, his future and his hope, there were Catholic priests who would not stop believing in Jesus' prayer to be realized in my Daddy. They were there when others left him. They believed that God could and would do something in my Daddy's life. And my father was a blessed believer waiting to burst forth from a decaying drunk. To this day, I am thankful to a Roman Catholic order of priests who love alcoholics and will not give up on them when others do. I take exception to their view of justification, or the way we are saved. But I do not take issue with anyone's faith that says, "Jesus' power to transform a human soul is greater than humanity's power to destroy it."

My friends, Jesus will not give up on you. He has prayed for you. He did not give up on Saul of Tarsus in his sin, though even when Saul became the Apostle Paul, even Christians couldn't believe he was the real deal. Jesus never gave up on him. He saw what he would be because He prayed for him. And I don't care if today you are too far gone in the minds of some. You are not too far gone for Jesus if He has prayed for you. The sin of your alcohol may have destroyed your liver and your relationships, but Jesus prayed for you! He trusts in you when no one else does! Your infidelity may have destroyed your marriage, but God led you to this place to hear that Jesus has prayed for you and He will build a life out of the ruins of your sin or someone's sin against you! He believes in His power to save and His certainty to draw you to Himself more than you do and more than others do because He loves you and He chose you in love! **You are a child that has a self-image of a loser, of a troublemaker, and you may have lost and your pain and your sin and the devil himself may have trapped you and you are a troublemaker.** But Jesus sees a saint being born again out of a sinner. And you will come to Him. For Jesus prayed for you.

So, if you are fearful of trusting or perhaps feel unable to trust, this is your day. Because to listen to Jesus praying for you tells you that He has taken the first step to you because He loves you. He prayed that you would hear and believe, before you were born, before He even died for you, and yes before you even trusted in Him. And so, no matter what you are facing, you can trust in Him. Yet how do you respond if you are gripped by fear or trapped in sin? Or addicted? Or lost in your pain? I read these words this week from Brennan Manning's wonderful book, *Ruthless Trust*: "To be grateful for an unanswered prayer, to give thanks in a state of interior desolation, to trust in the love of God in the face of the marvels, cruel circumstances, obscenities, and commonplaces of life is to whisper a doxology in the darkness."

I will tell you about a doxology in the darkness, not a Psalm of praise, but a whispered song of trust. There is a pastor who lives and ministers in Seattle, Washington. I read of an encounter this pastor had one Sunday with a high-profile couple in his church who were sitting with their Down syndrome baby. He sensed that they were uncomfortable with the baby in worship and seemed to just try to get to the door as quickly as possible. He saw them there and asked them if they would wait for him to finish greeting the people and then meet with him in his office. They were confused and even uncomfortable, but they waited and met him in his office. There he asked if he could hold the baby. He took the child into his arms and began to sob. He looked into their eyes and asked them, "Do you have any idea of the gift God has given you in this child?" The parents were confused and even hurt. But the pastor went on, as he held the baby close: "Two years ago, my three-year-old daughter, Sylvia, died with Down syndrome. We have four other children, so we know the blessing that kids can be. Yet the most precious gift we've ever received in our entire lives has been Sylvia. In her uninhibited expression of affection, she revealed to us the face of God as no other human being ever has. Treasure this child, for he will lead you into the heart of God." From that day forward, I read that the parents began to brag about their little one.[25]

Why do I tell you that story? Because I believe it illustrates how God brings us to trust Him. He does it not by our expectations for the Messiah we think we want. But from the far reaches of doubt and despair that lead us to the Savior we need. We best believe not from our positions of strength, but out of weakness. We even cradle our weaknesses—the broken dreams, the unexpected illness, the abandonment, the failure—because in our weakness we see the heart of God. In our weakness in sin, we see a Savior who prayed for us, died for us, and rose again for us. And it is in His life, His prayer for us, His trusting heart for us, that we come to know that we can trust Him or trust Him again.

So, whatever you think is keeping you from Jesus is likely the thing that He is using to bring you to Him. You see this is possible, because of the deep, deep love of Jesus. For so we read in John 17. He prayed for you. Will you now trust in Him that today His prayer is answered once and for all in your life? Will you pray with me? As your head is bowed, I want you to name the pain. I want you to name the sorrow, even if that sorrow is fear to follow. And I want you to name it before Jesus right now as we pray.

PRAYER: LORD, I THANK YOU that You are for me and not against me. I thank You that the painful and even sinful things that I have named in my heart, that I have confessed, cannot keep You from me or me from You, because You have prayed for me. Lord, I thank You for the Cross, where pain gives birth to the heart and plan of God, the resurrection of Jesus. And I ask You, who have prayed for me, to come and open my heart and help me to believe in You, to trust in You like never before, and to follow You like never before. I know You will answer this prayer for I pray in the Name of the One who has prayed for me, even Jesus Christ. Amen. And Amen.

"A providence is shaping our ends; a plan is developing in our lives; God is making all things work together for good."

—F. B. Meyer

"GOD'S PROVIDENCE IN THE BOOK OF ACTS"*

So when they had come together, they asked him, "Lord, will you at this time restore the kingdom to Israel?" He said to them, "It is not for you to know times or seasons which the Father has fixed by his own authority. But you shall receive power when the Holy Spirit has come upon you; and you shall be my witnesses in Jerusalem and in all Judea and Samaria and to the end of the earth." Acts 1:6-8 (ESV)

Our word "Providence" is a compound of two Latin words, *pro* and *video*. Its basic meaning is "foresight," and in the context of our faith it means: God is guiding events for the sake of accomplishing His purpose. He has fixed the times and the places by His own authority, just as it says in the first chapter of Acts. The Father knows, and for His children, those who cling to Him in trust, that is enough. But we also need to take careful note of something else that is *not* included in this definition. It does not say that things are getting better for the Church every day. Nor does it promise that Christians will always be protected from suffering.

---

* Preached by Mr. Fred Guyette at Erskine Theological Seminary in Fall, 1998. Theme: "Providence" is the doctrine that says: God has a plan for salvation and He is working His purposes out. In the Book of Acts there are many characters—Peter, Gamaliel, Stephen, Phillip, Cornelius, Paul—but God Himself is the one who is driving the action.

The Providence of God is a central theme in The Acts of the Apostles.[26] Look with me, please, at one of the first major speeches given in Acts, in chapter two, and notice what Peter says in verse twenty-three about Jesus' crucifixion. Peter says that the crucifixion occurred as part of God's *"definite plan and foreknowledge."* And now let's turn to chapter four and verse twenty-eight, where the early Christian community prayerfully acknowledged to God that the plot against Jesus which led to His death was *"whatever Thy hand and Thy plan had predestined to take place."*

In the fifth chapter of Acts, when the apostles are brought before the Sanhedrin for preaching and teaching about Jesus, Gamaliel, a leader of the Pharisees, advises the council to leave them alone. Gamaliel gives this as the reason why: because *"If this plan is of men, it will come to nothing. But if it is of God, you will not be able to overthrow them, lest perhaps you be found fighting against God"* (Acts 5:38-39).

Now when Paul is given a chance to speak in public about the Christian faith in Acts 13, he provides an overview of salvation history. Paul says that God's plan for salvation began with the Patriarchs in Genesis. God made a covenant with Abraham, Isaac, and Jacob. When their descendants were forced into slavery in Egypt, God brought them out of bondage. He led them through the wilderness with a pillar of cloud by day and a pillar of fire by night, and then He gave them a good land. Soon after they settled in the land, however, their society descended into a long period of violence and moral chaos, which is described in the Book of Judges. The people of Israel hoped that King Saul's reign would make the situation better, but after some initial success, Saul's overall reign was a disappointment and a failure. David eventually became the king of Israel and this is important in Paul's estimation, not because David himself was a perfect king—far from it—but because God's promise of a coming Messiah was made to the house of David. That, too, was part of God's plan for the future (Acts 13:22-23).

"The plan of God" is again referred to in Acts 20. Paul is about to get on a boat and sail away from Miletus, because he felt that God wanted him to go and preach in other cities, so that the gospel might spread further abroad. For three years he had been teaching in Ephesus and Miletus. The people there were very dear to his heart and this departure was especially hard for him. In verse 20:27 he says that all during that three-year period, *"I did not shrink from proclaiming to you the entire plan of God."*

In addition to these five passages in which "the plan of God" is prominent, we often encounter the words *"it is necessary"* or *"we must"* in Luke and Acts, too. The Greek word for this is *dei*.[27] The use of this word is an important clue if we want to understand what the Book of Acts says about the fulfillment of God's plan. Here are ten places in Luke and Acts where we find this word *dei*.

> "I **must** be about my Father's business," says Jesus when He is twelve years old, in The Temple (Luke 2:49).

> Jesus says, *"I **must** preach the good news of the kingdom of God to the other cities also; for I was sent for this purpose"* (Luke 4:43).

> Jesus tells Zacchaeus to come down from his perch in the tree, *"For I **must** stay at your house today"* (Luke 19:5).

> *"The Son of man **must** suffer many things, and be rejected by the elders and chief priests and scribes, and be killed, and on the third day be raised"* (Luke 9:22).

> Repentance and the forgiveness of sins **must** be preached in Christ's name to all nations (Luke 24:47).

> Scripture **must** be fulfilled (Acts 1:16).

> The council strictly charges the apostles not to teach others about Jesus anymore, but they say, *"We **must** obey God rather than men"* (Acts 5:29).

Paul **must** carry the Lord's name before the Gentiles (Acts 9:6-16).

*"Take courage, for as you have testified about me at Jerusalem, so you **must** bear witness also at Rome"* (Acts 23:11).

God sent an angel to speak to Paul: *"Do not be afraid; you **must** stand before Caesar; and lo, God has granted you all those who sail with you"* (Acts 27:24).

One way in which the apostles "bear witness" in Acts is through public speeches. We find sixteen major speeches in Acts.[28] Most frequent are the speeches delivered by Peter (six) and Paul (eight). Stephen and James each give one major speech. And a careful reading shows us that these preachers do not spend a lot of time deliberating—Shall I accept this invitation to speak or not?—rather, the situation simply *demands* that they speak.[29] (1) Peter is compelled to preach at Pentecost in the second chapter of Acts in order to explain the unexpected things that the Holy Spirit is doing in their midst; (2) Peter must speak again after the healing of the lame man in Acts 3:11, because the crowd is wondering how this wonderful thing came to pass; (3) and he is required to speak yet again in response to the charges that are brought against him at the Sanhedrin (Acts 4:8-11; 5:29-32).

Stephen, too, is forced to give an account of his faith in response to the accusation that he spoke against The Temple (Acts 6). And Paul is miraculously called and chosen to proclaim the good news (Acts 9), in spite of his most zealous persecution of the Christian community. In fact, some of the first-century Christians were afraid that Paul's conversion was not genuine, that he was only trying to join them as a spy who meant to gather information about them and harm them further. It took some time for them to accept Paul and to understand that he truly had been called by God, and that God had given him a role to play in His kingdom.

So, the preaching in Acts is initiated by circumstances outside the control of the disciples. Why do these things happen? Because this is the mission of God.[30] He is the agent, the plan is His, and He is the one who directs the action in The Book of Acts. In His Providence, God is guiding these events to bring His purpose to fulfillment.

Let's return for a moment to the first chapter of Acts with the Providence of God in mind, and recall what Jesus said to the disciples who were gathered there in Jerusalem: *"You shall be my witnesses in Jerusalem and in all Judea and Samaria and to the end of the earth"* (Acts 1:8). So, one of the first things that happens after that is the coming of the Holy Spirit. Do you remember what happened at the Tower of Babel, how humankind was scattered and misunderstanding abounded because everyone was speaking a different language? That is a good background to help us comprehend what is happening in the second chapter of Acts—The Holy Spirit is making it possible for people who have been divided to come together and understand each other in a new way. What God promised in the time of the prophet Joel has been brought to fulfillment:

> *I will pour out of my Spirit upon all flesh: and your sons and your daughters shall prophesy, and your young men shall see visions, and your old men shall dream dreams: And on my servants and on my handmaidens I will pour out in those days of my Spirit; and they shall prophesy: And I will shew wonders in heaven above, and signs in the earth beneath; blood, and fire, and vapour of smoke: The sun shall be turned into darkness, and the moon into blood, before the great and notable day of the Lord come: And it shall come to pass, that whosoever shall call on the name of the Lord shall be saved.* Joel 2:28-32 (KJV)

In all the excitement of Pentecost we tend to overlook that one word in Joel: "whosoever." Why is it so important? Because for the most part, up until the day of Pentecost, salvation was limited to one group—the people of Israel. But in Acts, the gospel is going to spread geographically and salvation is going to be offered to everyone, regardless of where they come from.[31]

In chapter seven of Acts, we read that Stephen delivered a long speech to the leaders of Jerusalem. If Stephen had wished to save his own skin, he could have soft-pedalled the message. But Stephen felt compelled to state the truth boldly. Jesus had come to his own people, the people who should have recognized what God was doing in their midst, and instead they arranged to have Jesus put to death on a cross. When the crowd heard this accusation, they became angry and stoned Stephen to death, which is why he is remembered as the first Christian martyr.[32]

We can understand, then, when Acts 8 tells us that many Christians left Jerusalem because of persecution. But what happens next? We hear about Philip going to Samaria and preaching the good news there, and how *"there was great joy in that city"* (Acts 8:8). Next, we see him preaching in Gaza, and after that he helped an Ethiopian court official understand what he had been reading in the prophet Isaiah. And after that Phillip kept on preaching in city after city until he came to Caesarea. So terrible persecution came and what was the result? The spread of the gospel.[33] Who could have predicted that Stephen's death would be the catalyst for this new development?

As for Peter, God spoke to him in a vision—this was not his own idea. God spoke to him in a vision and he went and found Cornelius, a Gentile who was a Roman soldier. Cornelius was in that group of Gentiles known as God-fearers.[34] The implication is that he had seen enough of Rome's moral decay and that he was drawn to the moral teachings of Moses, though he had to remain something of an outsider to the synagogue. But Peter is sent to him and he tells him about Jesus and then Cornelius is baptized. No one could have predicted that these wonderful things would happen after that first wave of persecution, when Stephen was killed and the Christians fled from Jerusalem. But God was working His purpose out.

At that very moment, one of the most zealous of the men who persecuted Christians—his name was Saul—was trying to enlarge the scope of violence against the Christian community. He had applied for letters that would authorize him to keep on pursuing the Christians who had fled to other cities (Acts 9:1-2). On the road to Damascus, however, he had an experience that changed the course of his life. After his conversion, Saul the persecutor of Christians became Paul, the most effective missionary in the early church.[35] Paul carried the good news of Jesus Christ to many other cities, *"even to the end of the earth,"* just as it had been predicted in Acts 1:8. Among Paul's letters is I Corinthians, with the famous "love chapter" I Corinthians 13, which speaks so beautifully of faith, hope, and love.

And again, no one could have predicted that—but that's how it is with God's Providence!

PRAYER: ALMIGHTY GOD, IN THE Book of Acts You show us that through Your Providence You opened the way of eternal life to every race and nation by the promised gift of Your Holy Spirit: Shed abroad this gift throughout the world by the preaching of the Gospel, that it may reach to the ends of the earth; through Jesus Christ our Lord, who lives and reigns with You, in the unity of the Holy Spirit, one God, for ever and ever Amen.

"God the great Creator of all things does uphold, direct, dispose, and govern all creatures, actions, and things, from the greatest even to the least, by His most wise and holy providence, according to His infallible foreknowledge, and the free and immutable counsel of His own will, to the praise of the glory of His wisdom, power, justice, goodness, and mercy."

– Westminster Confession of Faith (V.1)

"THE SECURITY IN GOD'S SOVEREIGNTY"*

When they were released, they went to their friends and reported what the chief priests and the elders had said to them. And when they heard it, they lifted their voices together to God and said, "Sovereign Lord, who made the heaven and the earth and the sea and everything in them, who through the mouth of our father David, your servant, said by the Holy Spirit,

'Why did the Gentiles rage,

and the peoples plot in vain?

The kings of the earth set themselves,

and the rulers were gathered together,

against the Lord and against his Anointed'—

---

* This is a new sermon written for *Celebration* by Dr. Mark Ross. Theme: Faith in God's sovereign control and guidance of all things enables us to persevere through the trials and tribulations of life.

> *for truly in this city there were gathered together against your holy servant Jesus, whom you anointed, both Herod and Pontius Pilate, along with the Gentiles and the peoples of Israel, to do whatever your hand and your plan had predestined to take place. And now, Lord, look upon their threats and grant to your servants to continue to speak your word with all boldness, while you stretch out your hand to heal, and signs and wonders are performed through the name of your holy servant Jesus." And when they had prayed, the place in which they were gathered together was shaken, and they were all filled with the Holy Spirit and continued to speak the word of God with boldness.* Acts 4:23-31 (ESV)

It was all coming true. What Jesus had promised was being fulfilled. The arrest and crucifixion of Jesus had nearly shattered the faith of His followers. Just the mention of these things when Jesus first predicted them had stirred Peter to rebuke Him, *"Far be it from you, Lord! This shall never happen to you"* (Matthew 16:22). But it did happen, and for a time the disciples were plunged into confusion and disbelief. Even the glorious resurrection of Jesus did not immediately banish all their doubts (Matthew 28:17).

Eventually, however, their faith became stable. Jesus was alive, and He had now ascended to heaven. The Holy Spirit had come with power, just as He had promised (Acts 1:8, 2:1ff.). They were beginning to fulfill their calling to be witnesses for Jesus Christ in the world. But now there were further fulfillments of what Jesus had spoken, ominous ones: those who had opposed Jesus were now opposing His followers. Jesus had said, *"If they persecuted me, they will also persecute you"* (John 15:20). Peter and John had been arrested for preaching in the name of Jesus, and the ruling council of the Jews had been called to meet over the matter. The same leading figures appear as when Jesus had been tried—Annas the high priest and Caiaphas (Acts 4:6; John 18:12-14, 24).[36] Dark and threatening clouds seem to be gathering above the new community of believers in Jerusalem.

But for now the council decides only to threaten Peter and John. The miracle they had performed in healing the lame beggar (Acts 3:1-10) had become well known in the city, so the council considered it unwise to proceed further against the apostles. Thus, having been warned and threatened, Peter and John are released. They return to their friends and report all that had taken place before the chief priests and the elders. The assembly of believers is moved to offer praise to God, and Luke records for us the words which they spoke. These words reveal to us the foundation of faith upon which they were standing as they faced the opposition which had come against them. These words provide a foundation upon which we too can stand as we face the opposition that comes against our witness, as well as any other challenges to our faith that may arise. Let us consider three things that are especially prominent in the faith of the early church as they persevered in faith against the opposition.

First, they were convinced of **the great power of God**. *"Sovereign Lord, who made the heaven and the earth and the sea and everything in them . . ."* (Acts 4:23). Their God is the maker of heaven and earth, and all that they contain. This is the first article of faith in the Apostles' Creed—"I believe in God the Father, Almighty, the maker of heaven and earth." This creed originated as a profession of faith made by those coming for baptism, and thus is expressed in the singular as a personal confession. The Nicene Creed was formulated by a church council, called to make a united confession against false teaching at the time (A.D. 325). It is thus framed as a corporate confession— "We believe in one God, the Father almighty, the maker of heaven and earth, and of all things visible and invisible." This confession is rooted in the revelation of God in the Old Testament— *"Our help is in the name of the LORD, who made heaven and earth"* (Psalm 124:8). It is the first truth that we are taught in the Bible—*"In the beginning, God created the heavens and the earth"* (Genesis 1:1).

This is a truth so familiar that its significance could easily be overlooked. If our God is the maker of heaven and earth, then He is supreme over every other power; for every other power has received its power from Him. Therefore, no power on earth can thwart Him. No enemy can overcome Him. If His hand is raised against us, none can deliver us. If His hand is raised to defend us, then none could overpower Him. The believers in Acts had little power to stand against the Jewish council, particularly when they are joined with support from the Roman authorities. But the church knew they did not stand alone against that power. They served the *"Sovereign Lord, who made the heaven and the earth and the sea and everything in them"* (Acts 4:24). They believed as David believed, when the Philistines seized him in Gath, *"In God, whose word I praise, in God I trust; I shall not be afraid. What can flesh do to me?"* (Psalm 56, title and v. 4).

Isaiah appealed to the great power of God demonstrated in creation when he spoke words of comfort for the people (Isaiah 40). God *"measured the waters in the hollow of his hand, and marked off the heavens with a span, enclosed the dust of the earth in a measure and weighed the mountains in scales and the hills in a balance?"* He called upon the people to lift up their eyes and look upon the stars, for God *"brings out their host by number, calling them all by name."* For by *"the greatness of his might, and because he is strong in power not one is missing"* (Isaiah 40:12, 26). If God can keep all the stars in the grip of His hand, He can also keep all His people in the grip of His hand, so that not one goes missing. Our help is in the name of the *"Sovereign Lord, who made the heaven and the earth and the sea and everything in them"* (Acts 4:23).

Second, let us consider **the revealed truth of God**. The confession of faith given in the passage is grounded in the Holy Scripture as the word of the Sovereign Lord— *"who through the mouth of our father David, your servant, said by the Holy Spirit"* (Acts 4:25). There follows a brief quotation from Psalm 2. But notice how this quotation is introduced. The words of Psalm 2 have come from the *"Sovereign Lord, who made the heaven and the earth and the sea and everything in them, who through the mouth of our father David, your servant, said by the Holy Spirit."* Psalm 2 has come to us from God. It has come to us through the mouth of David. It has come to us through the mouth of David by the Holy

Spirit. God did not speak it directly out of heaven. He did not shake the heavens and the earth by His voice. But He spoke these words nonetheless, and what we have in Psalm 2, as in all the Bible, are His words, even as they are David's words too.

This is the doctrine of Scripture taught in all the Bible. Peter teaches it in his second letter— *"knowing this first of all, that no prophecy of Scripture comes from someone's own interpretation. For no prophecy was ever produced by the will of man, but men spoke from God as they were carried along by the Holy Spirit"* (II Peter 1:20, 21). Thus, when Isaiah foretold the virgin birth of Christ, the Lord Himself was speaking, as Matthew tells us— *"all this took place to fulfill what the Lord had spoken by the prophet"* (Matthew 1:21). This is why Paul says, *"All Scripture is breathed out by God"* (II Timothy 3:16). God's giving of His word utilized the means of human authorship, both speaking and writing, but His sovereign determination was not merely an influence exerted on the writer, but continued all the way down to the letters on the page. Peter tells us about the process which gave us the Scriptures— *"men spoke from God as they were carried along by the Holy Spirit."* Paul tells us about the finished product— *"All Scripture is breathed out by God."*

At one time ancient Israel did possess words that God himself had written, the Ten Commandments. They were engraved upon two tablets of stone, written by the finger of God (Exodus 24:12, 31:18). But the Ten Commandments were not all the words which God gave to Israel on Mount Sinai. There were many other words spoken privately to Moses and then he wrote them down. Then Moses read the words to the people, and they received them as the words of God, *"All the words that the LORD has spoken we will do"* (Exodus 24:3, 7). What Moses had written down was just as much the word of God as the two tablets written by the finger of God. When Ezra the scribe read this law to the people centuries later, he was reading *"the law of Moses that the LORD had commanded Israel"* (Nehemiah 8:1).

Many more examples could be provided which demonstrate that the words of the Holy Scriptures are the words of God. We have in them the revealed truth of God, to guide and direct us in our service to God, to uphold and sustain us in that service. So it is that the early church in Acts depended on the Scriptures as they faced the opposition of the Jewish council. In Psalm 2 they saw that the opposition they were facing was but one more instance of the opposition prophesied in the Holy Scriptures, *"against the Lord and against his Anointed"* (v. 26). Looking to that Psalm, they would not only find that the opposition they face is to be expected, but that the triumph of the Lord's Anointed is also to be expected—*"You shall break them with a rod of iron and dash them in pieces like a potter's vessel"* (Psalm 2:9). Luke demonstrates that victory in his book of Acts as he traces the progress of the gospel in a short sample of church history, using a part of the story to forecast the whole. He chronicles the spread of the gospel from Jerusalem (Acts 1-7), to Judea and Samaria (Acts 7-12), and on to Rome (Acts 13-28). He concludes his book by telling that Paul stayed in Rome two full years, welcoming all who came to him, proclaiming the kingdom of God, and teaching about the Lord Jesus Christ with all boldness and without hindrance (Acts 28:30, 31). Nothing can stop the advance of the gospel!

The Holy Scriptures provide us with the revealed truth of God by which He sustains His people as the manna sustained Israel in the wilderness, for man does not live by bread alone, but by *"every word that comes from the mouth of the LORD"* (Deuteronomy 8:3). Psalm 2 was sustaining the church as it saw in the deliverance of Peter and John from the Jewish council that the Sovereign Lord was standing by His word. But they saw this supremely in the work of Christ upon the cross, which brings us to the consideration of another element in the faith of the early church.

Third, the early church believed in **the all-embracing providence of God**. When we speak of God's providence, we mean that God directs and governs all the events of history for the accomplishment of His purposes. This doctrine is aptly summarized in the Westminster Confession of Faith (V.1): "God the great Creator of all things does uphold, direct, dispose, and govern all creatures, actions, and things, from the greatest even to the least, by His most wise and holy providence, according to His infallible foreknowledge, and the free and immutable counsel of His own will, to the praise of the glory of His wisdom, power, justice, goodness, and mercy." God did not make the world and then leave it to run on its own. He directs and governs all that happens for the accomplishment of His purposes.

The truth of Psalm 2 was seen by the early church not only in the recent conflict between the church and Jewish council, and in the deliverance of Peter and John, but supremely manifested in the accomplishment of God's saving purposes in the cross of Jesus Christ—*"for truly in this city there were gathered together against your holy servant Jesus, who you anointed, both Herod and Pontius Pilate, along with the Gentiles and the people of Israel, to do whatever your hand and your purpose predestined to take place"* (Acts 4:27, 28). The enemies of the gospel had come in force against the Lord's Anointed, Jesus; but for all their rage and all their fury, what happened was only what the Lord's hand and the Lord's plan had predestined to occur. It was all under His control and according to His plan. Nothing was outside His all-embracing providence. There were the principal powers of the place, both Herod and Pontius Pilate; and there were all the subordinate actors, the Gentiles and the peoples of Israel. They all had their own goals and made their own choices; yet what happened was what God's hand and God's plan had predestined to take place. Nothing was left to chance.

Peter made the same point in his Pentecost sermon: *"This Jesus, delivered up according to the definite plan and foreknowledge of God, you crucified by the hands of lawless men"* (Acts 2:23). Notice how Peter reports the sovereign determination of God in all that happened, while at the same time making clear that those who perpetrated the crucifixion were lawless men, and thus fully responsible for their wicked deeds. No divine compulsion was upon these people coercing them against their wills. They all acted in accordance with their wills. Jesus likewise joined these two concepts together when he declared, *"For the Son of Man goes as it has been determined, but woe to that man by whom he is betrayed"* (Luke 22:22). Judas did exactly what had been determined by

God's eternal plan, yet he did it by his own wicked choice, as he himself admitted, *"I have sinned by betraying innocent blood"* (Matthew 27:4).

The Scriptures do not teach the absolute sovereignty of God over all things by denying that human beings (or angels) make real choices and are responsible for them. The doctrine of divine sovereignty is not fatalism, the idea that what will be, will be, regardless of what we do. No, what we do is part of the nexus of causes at work in the world, but all the causes are sovereignly ordered by God, for the accomplishment of His own purposes. As Psalm 2 teaches, *"the nations rage and the peoples plot in vain, the kings of the earth set themselves, and the rulers take counsel together, against the Lord and against his Anointed; yet the Lord sits in heaven and laughs, and holds them in derision"* (Psalm 2:1-4). What will be is what God has determined will be, and that is good news for all who trust in Him. It is bad news for all who oppose Him, very bad news indeed.

The Sovereign Lord was wholly in control of all that happened when Christ was crucified, and He is wholly in control of all that has happened and will happen since. If this God promises that for those who love God all things work together for good (Romans 8:28), we can be sure it will be so. With Job we can confess, *"I know that you can do all things, and that no purpose of yours can be thwarted"* (Job 42:2). It makes sense to pray to a God like this, for He has sovereign power to grant what His people seek. Since He has revealed His truth to us, we know what we ought to seek from Him. Because His providence embraces all that happens, we can be sure that what He has promised, and what He has planned, will surely come to pass.

Prayer is exactly what we find the early church doing as they reflect upon the great power of God, the revealed truth of God, and the all-embracing providence of God. They know that opposition to the gospel is sure to come, and they know they have been called to bear witness to the gospel. In the face of such opposition, they seek to be faithful to the purposes of God, speaking boldly the word of God. Their prayer rose up to God, and He granted their request—*"And when they had prayed, the place in which they were gathered together was shaken, and they were all filled with the Holy Spirit and continued to speak the word of God with boldness"* (Acts 4:31).

Our own prayers, and our own life, should be stirred by what we find in this passage. Our faith must be grounded in the same truths. We must trust in **the great power of God**, for He has made the heaven and the earth and the sea and everything in them. We must trust in **the revealed truth of God**, for we do not live by bread alone, but by every word that comes from the mouth of God. We must trust in **the all-embracing providence of God**, for all that happens is ordered by Him for the accomplishment of His sovereign purposes. What He has promised will be fulfilled. What He has decreed will come to pass. He has put *"in Zion a stone, a cornerstone chosen and precious, and whoever believes in him will not be put to shame"* (I Peter 2:6). Thanks be to God!

PRAYER: ALMIGHTY GOD AND HEAVENLY Father, You are the God of yesterday, today, and tomorrow, holding all things in Your hands and directing all Your creatures and all their actions. Grant that we, Your people, will rest in the confidence that we are not alone, but at every moment live in the certainty that You are working in our lives to accomplish Your purposes and to bring us to Your appointed ends, through Jesus Christ our Lord, Amen.

"Our true wisdom is to embrace with meek docility, and without reservation, whatever the holy scriptures have delivered."

—John Calvin

"SOLA SCRIPTURA: GOD'S MIRACLE BOOK!"*

Comfort, comfort my people, says your God. Speak tenderly to Jerusalem, and proclaim to her that her hard service has been completed, that her sin has been paid for, that she has received from the Lord's hand double for all her sins. A voice of one calling: "In the wilderness prepare the way for the Lord; make straight in the desert a highway for our God. Every valley shall be raised up, every mountain and hill made low; the rough ground shall become level, the rugged places a plain. And the glory of the Lord will be revealed, and all people will see it together. For the mouth of the Lord has spoken." A voice says, "Cry out." And I said, "What shall I cry?" "All people are like grass, and all their faithfulness is like the flowers of the field. The grass withers and the flowers fall, because the breath of the Lord blows on them. Surely the people are grass. The grass withers and the flowers fall, but the word of our God endures forever." Isaiah 40:1-8 (NIV)

But as for you, continue in what you have learned and have become convinced of, because you know those from whom you learned it, and how from infancy you have known the Holy Scriptures, which

---

* Preached by Dr. Leslie Holmes at Covenant of Grace ARP Church on November 12, 2017. Theme: The Bible, the infallible and inerrant Word of God, is the most amazing book ever written!

are able to make you wise for salvation through faith in Christ Jesus.
All Scripture is God-breathed and is useful for teaching, rebuking,
correcting and training in righteousness, so that the servant of God
may be thoroughly equipped for every good work. II Timothy
3:14-17 (NIV)

Just over 500 years ago, an Augustinian friar named Martin Luther
posted his Ninety-Five Theses on All Saints Church door in Wittenberg,
Germany. In so doing, he kindled a flame that turned around the
history of the Christian Church and the entire Western world. At the
heart of Reformation thinking are these five Latin pillars called "The
Five Solas:" Sola fide reminds us that we are saved through faith alone!
Sola gratia tells us that we are saved by grace alone! Sola Christus is our
reminder that Christ alone saves us! Soli Deo Gloria states the purpose
for our being saved. We are saved to glorify God alone! These first four
Solas stand on a fifth Sola, which is Sola Scriptura! Sola Scriptura tells
us that all truth is God's truth and that He has revealed His truth in
Scripture alone! Martin Luther said, "A simple layman armed with
Scripture is greater than the mightiest pope without it!" I want to help
you understand the importance of the Bible in our day, and will do so
by looking at four key words.

The first word is **Foundation**. In II Timothy chapter three, the
Apostle Paul warns Timothy to be on the alert because an impend-
ing perilous time of deepening apostasy looms on the horizon. Paul
advises Timothy that if he will stay straight in his thinking, he will
remember that *"All Scripture is God-breathed and is useful for teaching,*
rebuking, correcting and training in righteousness, so that the servant of
God may be thoroughly equipped for every good work" (II Timothy 3:16).
He uses a compound Greek word *theopneustos.* This word says that all
Scripture is *"God-breathed."* That is the Bible's foundation! The Apostle
Peter echoes this sentiment when he writes, *"No prophecy was ever*
produced by the will of man, but men spoke from God as they were carried
along by the Holy Spirit" (II Peter 1:21).

Hence, at Erskine Theological Seminary we affirm that the Bible alone, only the Bible, and the Bible in its entirety is the Word of God written, and it is therefore without error in the autographs, or the original documents as written by *"holy men of God"* (II Peter 1:22, KJV).

The second word is **Formation**. With the word "formation," we are speaking about how the Scriptures were formed, or how they came to exist. Let me ask you a few questions about your great-grandfather. What was his full legal name? What was his profession? What color were his eyes? More important, what did he believe concerning religion? What did he believe about Jesus? Knowing the answers to these questions would place you in a very select group of people. But, come back with me three more generations: What about your great-grandfather's great-grandfather? What was his full legal name? What was his profession? What color were his eyes? More important, what did he believe concerning religion? What did he think about Jesus? Now, come back with me three more generations: Let's talk about your great-grandfather's great-grandfather's great-grandfather? What was his full legal name? What was his profession? What color were his eyes? More important, what did he believe concerning religion? What were his thoughts concerning Jesus Christ? You may say, "Well, we have a family tree with all these people but it doesn't have all that kind of detail." That's just nine generations!

Here is a more important question: What do you believe concerning religion? What about Jesus? Who is He to you? Do you know Him through religion? Or, through relationship? To echo the amazing question our Lord asked the Pharisees *"What do you think about the Christ? Whose son is he?"* (Matthew 22:42). That is the most important question anyone can ever ask or ever answer. How do you answer it? Christ once asked His disciples, *"Who do you say that I am?"* (Matthew 16:15). It was the same question using slightly different words and the biggest question He ever asked them, second to none. It is the biggest question you will ever answer, too, so listen carefully to the answer, as blurted out by Peter that day. Peter responded, *"You are the Christ, the Son of the living God"* (Matthew 16:16). That answer would impact Peter's eternity, just as surely as your answer will impact your eternity. Can you give Peter's answer?

I asked about nine generations in your family tree for a reason. I doubt that you can go back that many generations in your family tree. Very few people could answer that question. I've never met anyone who could go into the kind of detail I was asking for three generations much less for nine generations. However, imagine: Here are sixty-six books written by forty different authors over sixty-four generations. That is seven times longer than I just asked you! These forty different authors come from unrelated backgrounds and they speak different languages and dialects. Among them you will find a king, a herdsman, a physician, a taxman, a theologian, a lawyer, a fisherman, and a Hebrew scholar. They have no access to e-mail, or telephone, or even snail-mail! In fact, most of them were not even aware that the others existed. Yet, from them we get a book with the complete harmony and unity of a perfectly crafted patchwork quilt. That is the Bible's formation story.

The third word is **Fashionable**. When I use the word "fashionable," I mean that the Bible is a book that is timeless, and its message is never out of date. Other books come and go, but this book we call the Bible is not the latest release from Oprah's Book Club or someone's book of the month. Consider these words from the longest Psalm, whose theme is the Bible's authority: *"Forever, O Lord, your word is firmly fixed in the heavens . . . . Long have I known from your testimonies that you have founded them forever . . . . The sum of your word is truth, and every one of your righteous rules endures forever"* (Psalm 119:89, 152, 160). Psalm 119, the longest of all the Psalms and, indeed, the longest chapter in the Bible, is what we sometimes call an "orphan" Psalm. We do not know who wrote it but we know its message. Its writer, apparently seeking sanctuary from his persecutors, finds strength by meditating on God's Word. C. S. Lewis said it reminds one of a fine piece of embroidery, done stitch by stitch. Each stitch is sewn in love, and each one describes how God's Word equips us to grow in godliness as we face life's persecutions and pressures. The Psalm is a call to walk by faith in the believability of what God says.

Three times, as we read this Psalm affirming the Scriptures, we find that word *"forever."* The psalmist wants us to know that this book is here to stay. He uses the Hebrew word *"leo-lam,"* which is found in Scripture 174 times and in every one of those times it speaks about permanence, changelessness, indestructibility. Isaiah uses the same word, so we might say that this is the psalmist's way of aligning his teaching with that of Isaiah when he says, *"The grass withers and the flowers fall, but the word of our God endures forever"* (Isaiah 40:8).

Leo-lam! Yes, read the pages of any history book and see how civilizations are transformed. We need no reminder in this era of the computer revolution that human knowledge grows today at a speed without precedent in all history and the rate keeps increasing. Some people at IBM believe that human knowledge will soon double not every twelve years, or every twelve days, but every twelve hours! Life moves on with amazing rapidity, but God's Miracle Book stands firmly "forever." There is an immutability, or stability, about the Bible that never has been and never will be undermined.

I am reminded of something that my Uncle Sam said to me one evening when I spoke with him about one of my college professors who took great delight in criticizing and undermining the Scriptures. My Uncle Sam responded, "For two thousand years no book has suffered more at the attempts of crackpots and kooks to take it down. The fact remains that all its critics eventually pass away in infamy, and the Bible still stands in all its glory. Despite their best efforts, not one of them has taken away the weight of a single word from it!" He was right! The Bible is fashionable. It is forevermore fashionable because it is the breathed-out Word of the eternal God Who never changes.

Fellowship is the fourth word that comes to my mind as I speak about the Bible because when God inspired this book He had one primary purpose in mind. He wanted us to know Him. This book says God is reaching out in love to each of us and that He is the kind of friend who would die for you. No! Actually, it's bigger even than that! He is the kind of friend who would allow His only begotten Son to die for us on Calvary's cross. For what would you allow your only son or daughter to die? God watched silently as His Son Jesus was falsely accused, punched, spat upon, and finally hung on the most despicable instrument of punishment that the Roman Empire could imagine—a cross! From that cross at Calvary, Jesus prayed, *"Father, forgive them, for they know not what they do"* (Luke 23:34). Here is the good news: That same Jesus Christ is, right now, ready to forgive you. No matter what you have done, when you confess it Jesus says, "I forgive you." The Bible says, *"If we confess our sins, he is faithful and just to forgive us our sins and to cleanse us from all unrighteousness"* (I John 1:9). Think about it: the One Who knows the very worst thing you have ever done or thought of doing loves you best of all and says He will forgive you! John writes, *"I write these things to you who believe in the name of the Son of God that you may know that you have eternal life"* (I John 5:13). Yes, God inspired the words on every page of the Bible to welcome you into fellowship with Himself.

Foundation! Formation! Fashionable! Fellowship! Four powerful words about the most amazing book ever written—the Bible! Four words that changed history for the Church and the whole western world! Four words that will change lives forever! These four words can change your life right now if you will take the message of this book to heart, repent of your sins and ask Jesus Christ into your life from this day forward.

PRAYER: DEAR HEAVENLY FATHER, YOU have richly blessed Your church with Your living Word, the only perfect rule of faith and practice. Grant that we will believe Your Word, trust in Your Word, and hear Your Word as it brings to us the Good News that Jesus died to save sinners like us. In Jesus' name we pray, Amen.

CONTRIBUTORS

Dr. Terry L. Eves is an Elder in the Presbyterian Church in America and Professor of Old Testament at Erskine Theological Seminary. He has taught Old Testament, New Testament, and Biblical languages at Calvin College, Westmont College, and Erskine College before joining the faculty at Erskine Theological Seminary. He is a graduate of Grace College, Westminster Theological Seminary, and is a Ph.D. graduate of the Dropsie College of Hebrew and Cognate Languages. He is serving, for the second time, on the PCA General Assembly Theological Examination Committee.

The **Reverend R. J. Gore Jr., D.Min., Ph.D.** is a minister in the Associate Reformed Presbyterian Church, author, retired United States Army Chaplain (Colonel), and presently serves as Dean and Professor of Systematic Theology and Ministry at Erskine Theological Seminary. He has served presbytery and synod in many capacities, including serving as chair of synod's Interchurch Relations Committee and was a synod representative to the ARPC's chaplain endorsing agencies for fifteen years. Gore is a graduate of Bob Jones University, Faith Theological Seminary, St. Charles Borromeo Seminary, the U.S. Army War College, and holds the D.Min. degree from Erskine Theological Seminary and the Ph.D. from Westminster Theological Seminary. He has done additional studies at Chestnut Hill College, Princeton Theological Seminary, Columbia Theological Seminary, Reformed Theological Seminary, and Calvin College and Theological Seminary.

Mr. Frederick W. Guyette is Reference Librarian and Assistant Professor of Library Science at Erskine Theological Seminary and has published a number of essays in various journals. He is a graduate of

Florida State University, the Pacific School of Religion, Florida State University (graduate school), and is an M.Div. graduate of Erskine Theological Seminary. Guyette has done additional graduate studies at the Graduate Theological Union, Erskine Theological Seminary, and the University of the South.

The **Reverend R. Leslie Holmes, D.Min., Ph.D.** is a minister in the Associate Reformed Presbyterian Church, author, conference speaker, magazine contributing editor, and currently serves as the Provost and John H. Leith Professor of Reformed Theology and Ministry at Erskine Theological Seminary. He has over forty years of pastoral experience, with churches from 60 to 4,000 in membership, and has taught at conferences and theological seminaries on six continents. Holmes is a graduate of the University of Mobile, Reformed Theological Seminary, and holds the D.Min. degree from Columbia Theological Seminary and the Ph.D. degree from École Supérieure Robert de Sorbon (France).

Dr. Dale W. Johnson is an Elder in the Presbyterian Church in America, author, and Professor of Church History at Erskine Theological Seminary. He annually leads a Reformation Studies tour to Germany and has taught at several colleges and seminaries. He is a graduate of Cedarville University, Covenant Theological Seminary, Florida Atlantic University, and is a Ph.D. graduate of Georgia State University. He has done additional studies at Oxford University and the University of St. Andrews.

The **Reverend John Paul Marr, Ph.D. (cand.)** is a minister in the Associate Reformed Presbyterian Church and currently pastors the Troy ARP Church. He has been a teaching assistant in Biblical Languages and currently serves as Assistant Dean and Adjunct Instructor in Divinity. He is a graduate of Ithaca College, Erskine Theological Seminary, and is now a candidate for the Ph.D. degree at the University of Aberdeen.

The **Reverend Loyd D. Melton, Ph.D.** is a minister in the Southern Baptist Convention and presently serves as the John Montgomery Bell Professor of New Testament and Director of the D.Min. program at

Erskine Theological Seminary. Melton has served as Pulpit Supply for the Cedar Springs ARP Church for thirty years and is the senior faculty member at the seminary. Melton is a graduate of Presbyterian College, Erskine Theological Seminary, and is a Ph.D. graduate of the Southern Baptist Theological Seminary. He has done additional studies at Hebrew Union College (Cincinnati) and Union Theological Seminary (NY).

The **Reverend Matthew S. Miller, D.Min. (cand.)** is a minister in the Associate Reformed Presbyterian Church, having most recently served as senior minister of the Greenville ARP Church in Greenville, SC. He has translated and edited theological works in French for Zurich Publishing. Currently he serves as Director of Erskine's Greenville Extension and is an Adjunct Instructor in Divinity at Erskine Theological Seminary. Miller is a graduate of Wake Forest University, Reformed Theological Seminary, Erskine Theological Seminary, and is a candidate for the Doctor of Ministry degree at Erskine Theological Seminary. He has done additional studies at Harvard Divinity School and the University of Lausanne, Switzerland

The **Reverend Michael A. Milton, Ph.D**. is a Presbyterian minister, author, composer, retired United States Army Chaplain (Colonel), and presently serves as the James H. Ragsdale Professor of Missions and Evangelism at Erskine Theological Seminary. He is also the President of Faith for Living and the D. James Kennedy Institute for Reformed Leadership. Milton has served as senior minister of the historic First Presbyterian Church of Chattanooga and has founded three other congregations. He is a graduate of MidAmerica Nazarene University, Knox Theological Seminary, the University of North Carolina at Chapel Hill, and holds the Ph.D. degree from the University of Wales.

The **Reverend Toney C. Parks, D.Min.** is a minister in the National Baptist Convention, senior pastor of the Mount Sinai Baptist Church, Greenville, SC (twenty-six years), and presently serves as Associate Professor of Ministry at Erskine Theological Seminary. He has served as President of the South Carolina Congress of Christian

Education, Moderator of the Enoree River Baptist Association, Chaplain of the Greenville City Police Department, and President and Co-founder of Family Outreach Community Services in Greenville, SC. Parks is a graduate of the University of South Carolina, Erskine Theological Seminary, and is a D.Min. graduate of Westminster Theological Seminary.

The **Reverend Max Rogland, Ph.D.** is a minister in the Presbyterian Church in America, author, pastor of the Rose Hill Presbyterian Church in Columbia, SC, and Associate Professor of Old Testament at Erskine Theological Seminary. Rogland is a graduate of the University of Washington, Covenant Theological Seminary, and is a Ph.D. graduate of the University of Leiden (the Netherlands).

The **Reverend Mark E. Ross, Ph.D.** is a minister in the Associate Reformed Presbyterian Church, author, lecturer, former associate minister, and presently serves as the First Presbyterian Church-John R. de Witt Professor of Systematic Theology at Erskine Theological Seminary. He has served presbytery and synod in many capacities, including serving as chair of synod's committee that produced the ARP Church's Directory of Public Worship. Ross is a graduate of the University of Pittsburgh, Pittsburgh Theological Seminary, and earned the Ph.D. degree at the University of Keele (United Kingdom).

The **Reverend George M. Schwab Sr., Ph.D.** is a minister in the Evangelical Presbyterian Church, author, and Professor of Old Testament at Erskine Theological Seminary. Schwab is a graduate of Drexel University, Westminster Theological Seminary, and holds the Ph.D. degree from Westminster Theological Seminary. He holds Certificates from the Christian Counseling and Educational Foundation.

ENDNOTES

1. James Dabhi, "Can Moses Be Interpreted as a Paradigmatic Leader?" *Jeevadhara* 42, (2012): 87-103.

2. John Calvin, *Harmony of the Law.*

3. John Calvin, *Harmony of the Law.*

4. W. Ross Blackburn, *The God Who Makes Himself Known: The Missionary Heart of the Book of Exodus,* 39.

5. James K. Hoffmeier, "The Arm of God Versus the Arm of Pharaoh in the Exodus Narratives," *Biblica* 67, no. 3 (1986): 378-387.

6. Michael Duggan, *The Covenant Renewal in Ezra-Nehemiah.*

7. John Calvin, *Commentary on Jeremiah and Lamentations.*

8. Quotation attributed to William Still.

9. The late Doug Culver was Erskine Seminary Professor of Old Testament and Hebrew, speaking in the aftermath of the terrorist attack of Sept 11, 2001.

10. G. H. Jones, *1 and 2 Kings,* 440.

11. Douglas Adams, *The Hitchhiker's Guide to the Galaxy,* chapter 27.

12. Ward H. Lamon, *The Life Of Abraham Lincoln From His Birth To His Inauguration As President,* 372.

13. G. K. Chesterton, *The Everlasting Man,* Book 2, chapter 6.

14. At the time of this publication, the new pastor of Mother Emmanuel ARP Church is Rev. Eric Manning, a graduate of Erskine Theological Seminary.

15. Quoted in Stephen G. Dempster, *Dominion and Dynasty: A Theology of the Hebrew Bible*, 19.

16. Eugene Peterson, *Answering God: The Psalms as Tools for Prayer*, 29.

17. D. A. Carson, *How Long, O Lord*, 65.

18. Ibid.

19. Ibid.

20. Brennan Manning, *Ruthless Trust: The Ragamuffin's Path to God*, 1st ed.

21. H. Richard Niebuhr, *Christ and Culture*, 1st ed.

22. Ibid., 18.

23. Ibid., 27.

24. See Job 1:7-11.

25. From my personal files; the names will remain anonymous.

26. John T. Squires, *The Plan of God in Luke-Acts*, 1-3.

27. Charles Cosgrove, "The Divine DEI in Luke-Acts: Investigations into the Lukan Understanding of God's Providence," *Novum Testamentum* 26, no. 2 (April 1984): 168-190.

28. Johan Ferreira, "The Plan of God and Preaching in Acts," *Evangelical Quarterly* 71 (1999): 209-216.

29. Kenneth Bass, "The Narrative and Rhetorical Use of Divine Necessity in Luke-Acts." *Journal of Biblical and Pneumatological Research* 1 (2009): 48-68.

30. Stephen Strauss, "The Purpose of Acts and the Mission of God." *Bibliotheca Sacra* 169, no. 676 (2012): 443-464.

31. I. Howard Marshall, "The Significance of Pentecost," *Scottish Journal of Theology* 30, no. 4 (1977): 347-369.

32. Michael Patella, "Do not hold this sin against them"—The Martyrdom of Stephen (Acts 7)," *Bible Today* 55, no. 3 (May 2017): 193-201.

33. Scott S. Cunningham, "Through Many Tribulations": *The Theology of Persecution in Luke-Acts.*

34. Martinus C. de Boer, "God-fearers in Luke-Acts." In *Luke's Literary Achievement: Collected Essays*, 50-71.

35. Brian Tabb, "Salvation, Spreading, and Suffering: God's Unfolding Plan in Luke-Acts," *Journal of the Evangelical Theological Society* 58, no. 1 (2015): 43-61.

36. Caiaphas, the son-in-law of Annas, is officially the high priest at this time, so far as the Romans were concerned, for they had usurped the power of appointing the high priest. Annas had been removed in AD 15, but he remained the dominant power even afterwards. This may be seen from the Scriptural narrative of Jesus' arrest. He was first taken to Annas (John 18:12-14), and then was sent to Caiaphas, to make things official before sending Jesus to Pilate (John 18:24, 28). Luke indicates the continuing power of Annas when he describes the beginning of Jesus' ministry as taking place "during the high priesthood of Annas and Caiaphas" (Luke 3:2), as if there were two high priests at the time. In the sense explained above, there were.

For more information about
Erskine Theological Seminary
&
Celebration
please visit:

www.seminary.erskine.edu
rgore@erskine.edu

For more information about
AMBASSADOR INTERNATIONAL
please visit:

www.ambassador-international.com
@AmbassadorIntl
www.facebook.com/AmbassadorIntl

*If you enjoyed this book, please consider leaving us a review on
Amazon, Goodreads, or our website.*